Fighter Pilot

McSCOTCH

First published in 1936 by George Routledge & Son Ltd.

This edition published in 2018 by Sharpe Books.

ISBN: 9781793044709

TABLE OF CONTENTS

THIS book consists of the reminiscences of an ordinary fighter pilot of the R.F.C. who had the privilege of serving in one of the leading Fighter Squadrons and who had the honour of being the friend of the supreme fighter of all the Air Forces, that indomitable and lovable patriot,
'MICK' MANNOCK, V.C., D.S.O., M.C.

CHAPTER ONE

ON a serenely warm afternoon at the end of May 1917 I was being whirled along the *pavé* road between St. Omer and Aire on my way to join 40 Squadron of the Royal Flying Corps. The road, one of those permanent monuments to the intentions of Napoleon, leading straight to the English Channel, was lined by tall poplar trees which appeared as if they were going to fall over us as the R.F.C. tender tore along at something like fifty miles an hour. The steel-studded tyres maintained a high-pitched whistle as they feverishly gripped the whinstone blocks of the road, the clear fresh country air sang in our ears.

The pilot sitting between the driver and myself, 'Melbourne' Basset, was the cause of the haste. He had been sent to St. Omer to collect me from the 'Pilots' Pool', and in explanation for allowing me only five minutes in which to pack my belongings had said:

"Got to get back quickly. Something 'on' tonight."

As the car sped along between the rows of trees he dropped into a morose silence, staring straight ahead of him as if there were something at the end of the road of which he was afraid. In reply to my questions about the squadron and the 'machines', he answered only in monosyllables. Poor Basset, something *was* going to happen but not until the next morning.

It was my first journey to the 'line', that magic and tragic word that embraced the whole of the battle areas of Northern France and Flanders.

On that road, along which so many were never to return, the taciturn attitude of my travelling companion gave me time to think. After two years in the infantry at home I had come to the conclusion that at twenty, with two years of very nondescript training mostly as a specialist in bombing and musketry, I was not in any way qualified to accept responsibility for the lives of a platoon of men. All through my training the thought of twenty-two lives depending on my word of command had appalled me and, on confiding my fears to a friend, I was given some very acceptable and practical advice. This friend, who had been sent to France in the first month of the war and who was killed in France the day before the Armistice, had said: "The right job for you is in the Flying Corps. Fellows like you that need 'holding down' can do ten times as much good in the air as you ever will on the ground."

Two or three more months passed without any sign of being sent overseas, so I had transferred to the Flying Corps. Even then the thought of having the life of an observer in my hands made me determine to become a single seater or 'scout' pilot; I wanted to fight alone, relieved of the knowledge that a mistake on my part would cost another fellow his life. Besides, the endorsement on my 'Training Brigade Transfer Card' written in red ink 'Rotary Scout Pilot' meant much more to me than the certainty that I was going to be clear of responsibilities. The title, an honourable one from 1916 to 1918, although meaningless nowadays, translated into modern terminology signifies a 'Single-seater fighter who is capable of flying aeroplanes with rotary engines'. Single-seaters were originally called 'scouts' because they were designed to act as the 'eyes' of the infantry; the latter, confined to the trenches, were, through the single-seater, given some knowledge of the enemy dispositions and movements.

By 1917, however, the term 'scout' no longer applied; reconnaissance work was carried out by two-seater machines, and single-seaters were relegated (or promoted) to the more aggressively active task of offensive and defensive fighting. The 'scouts' fought in the vanguard of every attack in 1917 and 1918; their spectacular work made them appear as the gladiators of the war, particularly after Captain Ball, the V.C., had brought the single-seater pilot into the limelight by demonstrating the destructive value of a spirited fighter. Every 'scout' was, at least, entitled to hope that the coveted decoration was already under his pillow. Until the end of the war the single-seater pilot waged an individual battle against the enemy, for even when with his flight or his squadron, his success and chances both of victory and life lay in his own hands and depended to a considerable extent on his own spirit and the intelligence he applied to his 'job' of shooting down the enemy machines.

So it was that on the way to joining 40 (Scout) Squadron at Bruay, I had a definite feeling of fulfilment. The red endorsement on my card had been the first part of my ambition. I was at last going to take my part in the Great War, to kill the country's enemies and to meet new friends, to live at such a 'pitch' that the memory of it is as fresh to-day as when it all happened. What it was really going to be like or what it was going to mean to me I had no suspicion. At any rate, there was no premonition, no fear in my mind, my only emotion was anticipation.

The car passed through one town, and on entering the market square of another, Lillers, Basset climbed out to dash into a bakery. He was in a terrific hurry, as if 'Cutty Sark' were on his heels, and when he came out carrying parcels of bread and cakes he almost gasped: "We ought to do it!"

The car continued its race along a now dusty road, while I wondered why Basset was in such unseemly haste, but his preoccupied manner discouraged questions. I was curious to know; to get a glimpse of what was 'going to happen'. Everything that had to do with war, the real war I mean, the war of killing, and the war that went on within the fellows' minds was a subject worthy of investigation, but it was not until several days later that I found out the reason for Basset's fear. One or two pilots had been suspected of evading patrols through subterfuges, and Basset, to prove that he did not belong to that gutless and fortunately rare type, was hurrying back so that he would be in time for a flight patrol, even when his early return meant inconvenience to me, to the driver, and risk to the car with its three occupants.

We stopped at a closed level crossing in Bruay; Basset took out his watch, glanced at it and immediately relaxed, "We've done it all right."

As we finally slowed down alongside an aerodrome on which four or five Nieuports were standing, he thanked the driver, jumped out, and hurried into one of the canvas Bessaneau hangars.

The camp was about a hundred yards up a lane on the left-hand side of the road and consisted of ten or eleven small brown canvas Armstrong huts surrounding a red ash tennis court with a large black wooden mess hut standing twenty yards away on the north side. There was a game in progress, and the sight of four fellows, three of whom were in flannels, playing an energetic game of tennis 'up the line' came as a great surprise to me. I had thought only of khaki and the duty side of fighting, not of the relaxation between times. The general impression surrounding the camp was that of a peaceful tennis club at home.

I asked one of the pilots who were sitting round in deck-chairs where I might find the Commanding Officer.

"You're the new fellow?" he asked. And on my admitting that I was he gave me a cheery welcoming smile.

"That's the C.O. over there," indicating a young rather florid-faced youth at the far side of the net. "But you had better not disturb him till the set is finished."

The latter, when the 'over' was finished, waved his racquet to me. "You the new pilot? See you later when we've won this set."

This informal greeting struck me as being unusual — no fuss, no formality.

The sun was beating down on the court and the perspiring players fought a well-contested game. Overhead the noise of five rotary engines almost deafened us as a flight fell into formation. It was the first time I had seen a whole flight of the same type of machine together and was fascinated by the aluminium-coated Nieuports circling round as they fell into a 'V'-formation behind a machine with streamers on the struts and tail. They were going out to fight, Basset was in one of them. It would soon be my turn.

When the set was finished, the C.O. came over to me and, after making fun of my long and (to an Englishman) rather unpronounceable Scotch name, asked me if I had ever flown a Nieuport.

On being told that I had, he called out to the others: "Come on, here's a fellow from Smith Barrie's squadron who has flown a Nieuport. Let's watch what he can do!"

This was another surprise; I was not even being allowed to unpack, find a hut, or to get into flying-togs, but was to be hurled forthwith into the air to 'show them what I could do'.

Major Smith Barrie commanded No. 1 Reserve Squadron at Gosport, a 'scout' instructional squadron which was regarded as the training centre for 'stunt pilots'! From the C.O.'s remarks it was obvious that he expected 'something' from me.

Mechanics dragged out a Nieuport, someone lent me a flying cap, and I climbed into the cockpit, confident that I was going to give a demonstration of my capabilities. It almost invariably happens that when this feeling predominates over caution the result is an anti-climax. Through the kindness of the adjutant at the 'Pilots' Pool' I had managed to borrow an old Nieuport at St. Omer and had put in five or six hours' flying, during which I had performed every possible evolution. The one 'stunt' that had beaten me was the 'loop but when I learnt that Captain Ball was reputed to 'have broken his heart' attempting to 'loop' a Nieuport the annoyance at my failure was not so acute.

There were many interesting features about the Nieuport. Her wing span was no more than twenty-seven feet, the upper plane being almost twice the breadth of the lower one. The sole support between the planes, apart from the centre section, was a 'V'- shaped strut on either side and, because of this and the fact that only two landing wires and two flying wires were necessary, the planes presented a smart and tidy appearance. The whole fuselage, planes and tail plane were painted with aluminium dope which merited her the name of 'Silver Hawk' from the infantry. The engine was a 110 h.p. Le Rhone, a nine-cylinder rotary engine, controlled by a 'throttle' lever, and a 'mixture' lever operated by the pilot's left hand.

With this double adjustment it often proved exceedingly difficult to obtain the correct firing mixture for an engine and until a pilot became accustomed to his own there was always some danger of 'choking' it and stopping the propeller. At St. Omer I had learnt that it required nearly three thousand feet of vertical dive to restart an engine; so that 'losing one's prop' close to the ground entailed a hurried landing. The top speed on the level was about 95 m.p.h., a speed which, to road hogs and pilots of modern aeroplanes, may appear ludicrous for a 'fighting machine', but in 1916 when the Nieuport was first brought into action against the German Fokker, this speed represented the fastest that was attainable by a war aeroplane.

Unlike modern aircraft built for pleasant flying, the war machine did not require to be stable. In fact, one of the reasons for the efficiency of the Nieuport was that she was inherently unstable. A pilot had to 'fly' all the time he was in the air for, immediately he relaxed his hold on the 'joy-stick' and rudder, she would push her snub nose up into the air and, after completing a turn of a 'roll', spin slowly and insistently to the ground. This proclivity made her an excellent fighting machine, for once a pilot understood these idiosyncrasies he could utilise them to assist in the carrying-out of quick manoeuvres. I doubt whether any war aircraft of either side ever surpassed the Nieuport in ease of control in the type of flying we had to employ in aerial 'dog fights'.

Such was the machine I was supposed to 'stunt' for the edification and amusement of seasoned war pilots.

The result was almost a fiasco; but it found me a friend.

In my haste to get into the air, I evidently did not pay sufficient attention to the throttle and mixture controls. When I had climbed to 1,000 feet the engine coughed, spluttered and, to my utter disgust, stopped altogether with one blade of the propeller standing defiantly straight up in front of me. At 1,000 feet there was no room to dive to restart the engine, so, determined that I should at least perform one of No. 1 Reserve Squadron's pet 'stunts', I allowed the Nieuport to stall gently and then, as her nose went down, kicked her into a spin.

At that time in England, except in No. 1 Squadron, to get into a 'spinning nose-dive' was regarded as certain death, and although it was occasionally used by war fliers when avoiding enemy scouts who had succeeded in getting above them, it was rarely practised close to the ground. The newspapers then always described it as 'Deadly Spinning Nose-dive', scaremongering which probably had its demoralising influence on many pilots who lacked confidence in themselves or their instructors. To get a machine out of a spin one had to do the opposite of what one would at first sight expect. As the machine was pointing to the ground the natural reaction was to pull the joy-stick back to raise her nose, but the only way to stop the spin was to push the stick forward as if for diving, and to wait until the machine turned the spinning nose-dive into a straight dive before straightening out. At No. 1 R.S. all of us had become so expert at this that we could land straight from the last turn of a spin.

Without the engine propelling her, the Nieuport, that afternoon, behaved like a perfect little lady. She dropped her nose gently, turned round into the first turn of the spin with an easy grace and, still properly under control, commenced to spin slowly to the ground. With only the sound of the air whistling past the struts and wires I felt perfectly happy, watching the ground swirling round underneath and rising to meet me. At the correct moment I eased the joystick forward, straightened out, and did a perfect landing on the middle of the aerodrome.

I waited for the mechanics to start the engine, but when they ran out to me one of them said: "I think the Major would like to speak to you, Sir." I had quite forgotten the effect the 'spin' might have on the onlookers and, much to my amazement, on approaching the C.O. he turned away from me and walked towards the road.

Hurrying after him I stammered: "I'm sorry, Sir," but with a wave of his hand to show he did not want to speak to me, he walked on. The other pilots avoided me, so, disconsolate, perplexed and annoyed, I strolled towards the hangar. The attitude of the C.O. seemed quite unreasonable. Admittedly I had failed to control an engine but I had certainly landed the machine whole.

Muttering rebelliously to myself, I caught sight of a tall weather-beaten pilot almost shaking with mirth. Anger nearly got the better of me; I glared at him until, nodding in the direction in which the C.O. had disappeared, he said:

"*He* hadn't much to say to you, had he?"

Something in his healthy ruggedness arrested me.

7

"No, it was a pretty miserable show, wasn't it?" I replied, wondering what devilment made this strange pilot laugh. "But why didn't he wait until I explained?"

"Because he was absolutely speechless. They all thought you were going 'plonk' into the ground. We don't like watching fellows kill themselves, and Tilney (the C.O.) looked away when he thought you were 'finished'."

At this his laughter burst out anew in hearty guffaws and when these had subsided he turned his searching blue eyes on me.

"Tell me, honour bright, did you shove her into that spin intentionally. I saw you kicking your rudder."

I told him it was a favourite stunt and asked: "Do you think he'll send me back for further instruction?"

"Not Pygmalion likely," he said emphatically, "not when he knows you did it intentionally." Then, as an afterthought: "You pulled her out of it very nicely. If you can handle a machine like that we want you in this squadron."

Ever afterwards I felt grateful to him for these friendly and encouraging words. They saved me my self-respect and at the same time showed me that he had a somewhat 'Puckish' sense of humour. In using 'not Pygmalion likely', he was bowing to authority which decreed that 'not bloody likely' was as unsuitable for an officers' mess as it was supposed to be in Bernard Shaw's play 'Pygmalion'. His quick sight had enabled him to observe the movements of my rudder and, seeing the consternation and horror on the faces of the others had caused him the keenest amusement. As we walked to the camp little did either of us dream that this same sense of humour was to save our nerves on many later occasions.

"But that was a pretty dud show of handling an engine," I remarked. "I simply couldn't get the mixture once she was in the air."

At this he looked serious. "I don't damned well wonder. That machine belongs to Jake Parry, and no one else in the squadron will take her up. In any case, the old crock is going back to the depot, that's why they sent you up in her."

He thought for a few seconds. "I've always told them they'll kill someone through sending fellows up on their first solo on the worst machine in the squadron. That's what shook their insides when they thought that that engine had put 'paid' to you."

This was the beginning of my friendship with Mannock. He was twenty-eight or twenty-nine, and had then been two months in France. Everything about him demonstrated his vitality, a strong, manly, yet human vitality. His alert brain was quick to elucidate a principle, and an unbroken courage and straightforward character forced him to take action where others would sit down uncomprehending. I was awed by his personality and the fact that he was evidently a seasoned war pilot.

We walked to the camp together and on reaching the first hut nearest the entrance he looked in:

"So here you are! in Blaxland's hut," he said to me, and to Blaxland who was sitting on the bed writing: "Here's your new mate, Blax. Look after him before he kills himself."

Blaxland was the one who had greeted me on my arrival, a quiet, good-natured pilot, possibly two or three years older than myself. His sedate manner created an impression of a dignity beyond his years and the moderation of his opinions and his quiet voice inspired us with respect.

Finlay, 'cheery-faced Finlay' as I called him afterwards because his cheery greeting in the morning was sufficient to soothe the worst of breakfast tempers, was the most efficient and unobtrusive orderly it was my luck to have. He had unpacked my belongings, and everything in the hut was in order; even to my shaving tackle standing on a shelf above an enamel wash-basin. Finlay's kindly attentions must have helped to brighten the lot of many pilots.

As Blaxland continued his letter-writing I sat down to write too, to tell my people all about my experiences, hoping that they would appreciate my joy at being 'up the line'. There was a romance, a spirit of adventure, secrecy, ambition and fatalism in the address — '40 Squadron, R.F.C., B.E.F., France'. After the departure of the flight, an air of peace had descended over the camp. We were only eleven miles from the front line and yet there were no signs of war, no excitement, no bombardments, no shell-holes. Bruay itself had appeared to be quite untouched by the war; children played in the streets; miners walked about in their blue pit clothes, the engines at the pit-head belched thin steam into the air, while above, the black smoke curled slowly from a tall chimney stack. I had expected ruins, and 'Tipperary'-singing soldiers; instead I had found peace. Possibly the war, the real devastating, detonating war was nearer than it appeared to be. I wanted to ask Blaxland but he was writing busily.

Dinner that night was a gloomy affair. I knew no one in the squadron, and Mannock, sitting with me at the foot of the table, was as grimly silent as he had been enthusiastically loquacious in the afternoon. Afterwards, feeling depressed, I retired to the hut to write another letter. '40 Squadron, R.F.C., B.E.F.'

The writing cheered me, and ten minutes later when Mannock came to the door I had almost forgotten my depression.

"Well, young fellah," he said, adopting a 'Pukka Sahib' accent, "like to take a constitutional with me?" and then in his natural voice, "Want a walk, Mac?"

There was a clear-cut, incisive timbre in his speech, not exactly Irish, but with the definite enunciation and pure vowel sounds of the Celt.

Thoroughly delighted at being 'noticed' again by the 'seasoned' pilot, I put on my belt and cap. Mannock had changed into slacks, and his pale yellow socks and tie showed that regulations regarding dress were slightly relaxed at the front. His forage cap, soft round the edge, was poised on his head in the recognised Beatty angle. His carriage was more alert and springy than it had been when wearing his heavy flying boots, but there was something ungainly in his walk, as if his ankles or knees were stiff. Why it was that on the first evening I should feel an overwhelming sympathy for him because of his walk I do not know. A man's step can reveal such a great deal of his character and emotions, but Mannock's method of walking puzzled me, filled me with a sense of pathos.

Much of his 'natural' ruggedness of the afternoon had disappeared and he had obviously shaved after dinner — a small trickle of blood was oozing out of a cut on his jaw. When I pointed this out to him as we walked along the dusty lane, he stopped, pulled out a yellow silk handkerchief of the same colour as his tie and carefully wiped the blood away, asking me, "Are you sure it's all gone?"

I laughed at his concern and remarked on his silk handkerchief. "Your women friends evidently remember you!"

He was silent as we came out on to the road and turned towards Bruay. His face was set with an almost painful expression, and I glanced at him covertly several times, waiting for him to speak.

Knowing him so well afterwards I can surmise what was going on in his mind as we passed the hangars. His thoughts probably were: 'This is a new fellow. His first impressions are going to be indelible. Wonder what type he is? Seems fairly decent, but I'll soon find out. Anyway, he's new and inexperienced, I'll give him the chance I've never had.'

His first question towards 'finding out' was typical of the way he attacked everything. "Are you a snob?" he fired at me, giving my face that same penetrating scrutiny as when asking me about the 'spin'.

"Snob? How do you mean?" I asked. "If you are thinking of social snobs, then I'm not. We each have our own particular forms of snobbery: about intellect, character, ability, honesty and, I suppose, courage."

"Well answered!" he exclaimed. "But snobbery is a nasty word, I only apply it to social and money snobbery — the empty social type particularly. There are so many damned social snobs about."

He then proceeded to fire question after question at me, about my home, my education, and my religious beliefs. This inquisitiveness might have aroused some antagonism in me had it not been accompanied by a directness and understanding that one rarely discovers so quickly in strangers. He wanted to estimate my character and my spirit, not my social position.

At a cross-roads we sat down on a grassy bank, and he told me some of his own life and beliefs. He had had very little education, and through the poor circumstances of his family had started work as an errand boy. He told me how he had envied youngsters who had had the opportunity of going to secondary schools and university, and on my remarking that social position and education did not count with those that *did* matter in the world, his bitterness welled up as he put his hand on my arm. "That's it, old boy. It isn't the school or the university, nor who your father is, that matters, it's what you've got in your head and your guts."

Having got this off his mind he rose with a new alertness. "Come on. We'll show them."

This was a stock phrase of his during the first two or three months of our friendship. It told me that he was anxious to prove to the world the real value of what was within him.

For several hundred yards we walked along in silence, then, abruptly, he threw another of his quick-fire questions at me.

"Do you womanise?"

Evidently I persuaded him that my attitude towards decent women was similar to his own, for when we reached an estaminet in the middle of the town he stopped:

"Now that I know something about you, come in here and have a drink, I'm going to introduce you to a very nice young girl."

"I don't mind having a drink," I replied, "but I'm not particularly keen on meeting 'girls'. Besides, I thought you weren't either!"

"Come on, you fathead," he said, taking my arm and dragging me to the door, "this isn't one of that sort. She's the youngest, prettiest, sweetest and most innocent young thing you ever met; why do you think I changed into slacks and shaved for the second time to-day?"

Inside the estaminet there were several Frenchmen sitting at tables.

'Monsieur' came forward to greet Mannock effusively and to take our orders.

"Deux champagnes avec cognac."

We sat down in a far corner, and as Monsieur was placing the drinks before us Mannock leant forward to whisper something which caused Monsieur to go to a curtained door and shout: "Odette."

All the Frenchmen at the other tables looked up, first at Monsieur, and then round at Mannock.

"Damned fool," the latter growled, "giving me away like that," and, as an afterthought, "These French people are supposed to be so discreet and diplomatic — but just see what he's done."

The appearance of a young fair-haired girl soon took the frown from his face. He beamed on her and, having introduced me as an '*ami*' and an '*aviateur fameux*' he promptly forgot my existence, and for nearly half an hour I had to listen to a disjointed conversation in broken English and French. Odette was no more than sixteen or seventeen, a really beautiful blonde with that ethereal look that only fair women can possess. I was not surprised at Mannock's admiration.

When we returned to the camp it was dark, and the other pilots were sitting round the tennis court listening to a table gramophone playing Beethoven's 'Seventh Symphony'.

The air was still and warm, and in the darkness the peaceful theme of the third movement intensified the quietude that had settled over the small encampment. The distant rumble of gunfire only increased the somnolent effect.

"'Ark at 'em up at Ypres," someone said, using the 'argot' of the Squadron. "'Ark at 'em."

This caused a discussion which showed signs of becoming heated, when Major Tilney told the offenders to be quiet while he put on the final record for the evening.

This started another argument. Some of the pilots, complaining that they had to listen to symphonies, classical music and such 'tripe' every night and that something more inspiring and fitting for the surroundings, such as the 'Bing Boys', should be played.

The C.O. compromised by putting on a 'Hawaiian Melody', and when the strains of the haunting tune had died away Blaxland yawned.

"We had better go to bed, I have to take you up the line at half-past six, so we'll have to be up early," he said to me.

For some reason, the stuffiness of the hut, excitement or the rumbling of the guns, I did not go to sleep for a long time.

The 'Pilots' Pool' at St. Omer seemed very far away, seemed almost as if it had belonged to another life. Even the drive in the tender with Basset, the quiet worried Australian, was but a distant memory, and so was my first flight over the aerodrome. The only part of the day that seemed at all vivid was the walk with Mannock. In those days of intensive training, uncertainty, and living-for-the-moment, with all their attendant superficialities and immoralities, it had been refreshing to find someone whose mind was of an enquiring nature, who, right in the midst of war, had the time and equanimity to consider the values of ideals and beliefs. From the vehemence of his outburst against snobbery I surmised that the treatment he had had because of his humble upbringing had something to do with his loneliness and desire for the companionship of a stranger.

Although he had not mentioned the war, my attitude towards 'service' had already undergone a metamorphosis; I had imagined a grim, determined struggle with no time for solid thoughts beyond those of destroying the enemy or of self-preservation. Instead, I had found a rare oasis of mental refreshment amidst the moral wilderness.

I fell asleep feeling more at home with my surroundings than I had done since my enlistment.

CHAPTER II

THE next morning I awoke in a new world. The quiet serenity of the previous evening had given place to bustle and the noise of Le Rhone engines 'revving' full out.

Finlay, the cheery one, was standing over me with a cup of tea in one hand and a plateful of biscuits in the other.

"Good morning, Sir," he greeted me. "You are due to leave the ground at six-thirty and it's now six."

Blaxland was sitting up in bed drinking his tea, and on Finlay's departure I could not refrain from remarking on the luxury of getting 'early-morning tea'. In the infantry we had been accustomed to washing, dressing, parading and doing an hour's 'physical jerks' before breakfast without any 'home comforts'.

In a few minutes Finlay returned with a jug of hot water which he emptied into the basin, laying the neatly folded towel on the side.

"Do your clothes require any attention, Sir?" he asked me.

Finlay had that quiet, confident manner that commanded respect. He employed none of the 'old soldier' tricks to which I had been accustomed; everything necessary as well as a lot that was not really essential was done by him as unobtrusively as possible.

While dressing, Blaxland showed me a map of the front, pointing out the different landmarks; two pyramid-like dumps at Auchel, a peculiarly shaped wood behind Vimy and the two reservoirs alongside the La Bassée Canal.

"These are the principal ones," he said, "but when you get over the lines you will be able to make your own notes. We are about eleven miles from the front line now — just far enough to let us get a comfortable height before we cross."

When we were in the air my eagerness to see the lines for the first time made me forget all about the landmarks. Blaxland climbed steadily towards the east and in six or seven minutes we were flying over raw earthworks and trenches that

15

stretched as far as the eye could see both to the north and the south. The ground, for miles on the east and west of these trenches, was pock-marked with shell-holes amidst which we could discern the crumbling walls of shell-blasted houses. Except for one town, Lens, there was no sign of civilisation underneath us, but Lens, although the streets and houses were well defined, showed no signs of peaceful occupation, no smoke from the bare chimney stacks, no traffic in the streets — a deserted town just behind the German lines.

As we climbed, our horizon gradually widened and I could see a smaller town to the north, La Bassée. We continued climbing towards a bank of clouds, on reaching which, having found it rather difficult to play 'follow the leader' without any obstacles in the way, I promptly 'lost' Blaxland. Presuming that he had intended ascending through the clouds, I looked about for him on top of them, but in vain; the vast expanse of shimmering cloud showed up no machine. Confidently expecting Blaxland to appear any minute, I continued on my route without heeding in which direction I was flying.

At the end of a quarter of an hour, Blaxland not having appeared, I descended through the cloud to look for him. To my dismay, when I again got a clear sight of the ground, the trenches were in the far distance and the Auchel dumps and Bethune reservoirs had disappeared. Nearer me than the shell-bespattered trenches was a line of newly cut earthworks that looked as if they had been built as a model. (This was the Hindenburg-Drocourt line about four miles on the German side.) I was examining them and wondering vaguely whether our side of the trenches was to the east or the west, when, nearly choking with astonishment, I heard violent explosions that appeared to encircle me. One of them in front of me was so close that within a second my machine was flying through the pungent black smoke. There was no doubt that the Germans occupied *that* side of the line.

This was my first taste of 'Archie' and, thoroughly scared, I put the nose of my machine down and scurried towards the trenches as quickly as possible, to the accompaniment of sharp cracks and 'thuds' behind me. Only when I was again on our side had I the courage to look back, to see a straggling row of Archie bursts strung out in fours and fives along the course I had flown.

On my right was an unmistakable machine, an F.E.2B., one of our bombing and observation two-seaters. Being new — and with a desire to let someone see I was 'at the Front', I flew close to the F.E., but on noticing the observer standing up to aim his Lewis gun at me, I flew underneath to let him see my circles. I did not then realise that, as I had approached him from the sunny side, he could not see my machine clearly enough to recognise it as British.

There was no sign of Blaxland nor of the Bethune reservoirs. I was in a strange part of the line with no idea whether I was north or south of the sector over which I had crossed. My invariable custom in England when in doubt as to which way to turn when I came to the coastline had been to fly for seven minutes in one direction, and if that proved to be wrong to return and fly in the other, climbing all the time so as to enlarge my view. Under the circumstances, I acted on the same principle, flying northwards first. Presently I espied four machines approaching from the east. When they came near enough to let me see their outlines I failed to recognise them, and considering it wiser to avoid them, turned west; for even had they been British they would probably have led me farther astray. I had descended to four thousand feet in my precipitate flight from Archie, so, climbing again, I saw the Auchel dumps many miles away to the north-west.

On reaching them, failing to see Bruay and finding that there were two aerodromes near the dumps, I landed to enquire the direction of 40's aerodrome.

When I ultimately arrived at Bruay it was two and three-quarter hours since my departure — longer than our supply of petrol was supposed to last; and Blaxland was much relieved to see me. There was a joke in the squadron that every new pilot who lost himself flew straight towards Berlin. On one of these instructional flights over the lines which took place just before my time, the experienced pilot who was forced to return without the pupil because of the latter's evident desire to fly east, when asked by the C.O. where the pupil was, replied, "Oh — him! — why, he's in Berlin by this time."

Failing to follow my leader and losing myself invalidated my first educational flight and, that afternoon, Blaxland again had the unpleasant duty of taking me up. This time, after some sympathetic coaching from him, I succeeded fairly well, and in the evening was posted to 'A' flight.

The flight was commanded by Captain Bath, a tall Canadian who, before the evening patrol, gave me a sound piece of advice: "If you lose the formation — it's quite easily done, fly west — but it's a line patrol and you should have the trenches to guide you." He took the precaution of examining my compass and then told me that I was to fly at the right-hand extremity of a 'V' formation.

One pilot, Walder, came over to my machine and switched off my engine which was ticking over, so that he could say, "If any Huns come down on you from behind, you dive straight underneath the formation — don't wait to let them *get* you."

We fell into formation at three thousand feet over the aerodrome, behind Captain Bath whose Nieuport could be quickly recognised by the three flight-commander's streamers attached to the struts and the rudder. To facilitate recognition of the deputy leader in case Bath had to leave the patrol, Walder's machine had a streamer on the rudder only. Captain Bath headed straight for the lines at Lens and on arriving there turned north directly above the clearly defined front-line trenches. Eleven thousand feet proved to be a comfortable height for the German Archie gunners, and Captain Bath's course was a series of dives to the north-east followed by climbing turns to the north-west. Despite this the Archie bursts kept pace with us and, scared by the explosions as well as finding it difficult to keep my position in the formation, I paid little attention to what was going on. We drew near a large town (Lille) and our leader wagged his planes from side to side. This, the recognised 'enemy in sight' sign, made me examine the air ahead of us and I saw a green and yellow two-seater, just as Captain Bath dived on it. I could see the flaming tracer bullets pouring from the guns of the two leading machines and the two-seater diving away from them. I did not see what happened to it.

The flight then turned south and climbed to fifteen thousand feet, which it reached at Lens before the second beat of the patrol commenced. Flying on the extreme right of the formation my machine was farthest east, and every time Captain Bath turned it was my misfortune to find myself amidst a burst of Archie. Finally, for some reason or other unknown to me at the time, the Archie ceased. I flew along quite confidently about a hundred feet above and to the rear of Walder; finding that I could keep formation much better than on the previous trip north, my confidence increased. 'Educational flights are over,' I thought; but something that happened a few minutes later dispelled this illusion. I heard a sudden tat-tat-tat of a machine-gun and saw trails of smoke passing my machine between me and the right wing-tip. Glancing round hastily, I caught sight of a pointed-nosed machine diving straight past my tail plane. No sooner had it disappeared than the tat-tatting was repeated and another storm of smoke streamers flew by. I turned right round this time, to see another one pulling up out of a dive. The pilot flew above me for a little bit but, to my disappointment, he turned off east. I could clearly see his black and white crosses and his small under-carriage wheels.

I afterwards understood how, quite unwittingly, I had done the right thing. The Germans in attacking in this way hoped that by so doing they would separate me from the flight; but by my remaining in the formation and not even diving underneath Walder, their tactics were foiled. Knowing this, the flight proceeded as if nothing had happened.

Having finished the patrol without further incident, Captain Bath turned away from the lines. This caused me some surprise, for the time had passed so quickly that I was under the impression we had not been over an hour in the air.

At Bruay we landed in turn, and on climbing out of my machine I found a heated argument taking place between Walder and Captain Bath. The former maintained that it was dangerous both to the pilot and to the flight to allow an inexperienced beginner to take up the rear position.

On examining my machine they found several bullet holes in the right wing, and while the other pilots were filling in their combat reports, Walder took me aside and asked me if I hadn't seen the Germans.

Walder was serious minded, but could not help showing his amusement on hearing the facts.

"But why on earth didn't you dive as I told you to?" he asked.

"I forgot, and I was too interested in seeing what a German machine looked like anyway," I replied.

He then gave me another bit of information. "Whenever you hear a machine-gun, you may bet there's someone firing at you."

This first official patrol 'up the line' amply demonstrated to me that my education was just beginning. In fact, almost every flight for several months revealed some new feature of aerial warfare to me. It was like going to school for the first time. The principal points about my first baptism of machine-gun fire were: that I did not see the German until after his bullets had missed me, and that, observing that someone was shooting at me, I made no attempt to get out of his line of fire.

We had no time to change for dinner as it was nearly eight o'clock and, hastily slipping off my flying boots, I hurried into the mess. Dinner was in progress, and on taking my place I looked round the table to recognise the pilots. Failing to find Basset there, I committed a terrible breach of fighting squadron etiquette by asking where he was. The pilot sitting next me said 'shush' while Mannock, opposite me, gave my foot a kick. When the lugubrious meal was over, Mannock, whose pet name I learnt was 'Mick', told me that Basset was in hospital with an explosive bullet in his leg. He also told me that as the spirits of the younger pilots had to be kept up we were strictly forbidden to mention a casualty at mealtime.

It took me some time to get to know the other pilots, and although there were only fourteen or fifteen of us, several 'disappeared' before I even knew their names. Of the others,

Bond, Redler, Hall, Godfrey, Lemon, Captain Allcock, Shaw, Parry, Captain Keen, Walder, Cudemore and New formed a hazy background to my first impressions of the squadron. The friendliness of Mannock, Blaxland, Walder and Lemon helped me to get over the difficulties of the first few days, and, with the mental stimulus obtained from my evening walks with Mannock, my attitude towards the 'war' underwent a change. The feeling of uncertainty and insecurity that had haunted me no longer persisted.

Much to the amusement of some of the older pilots I spent a good deal of my spare time, and money, in decorating the brown canvas Armstrong hut with blue cretonne. To do so in one's first few days with a fighter squadron was the pinnacle of optimism. Anyway, Blaxland and I lived in comfort inside an attractive hut and, had it not been for the earwigs which abounded in the interior, we might have been considered 'civilised'.

At that time Mannock very rarely spoke of the actual fighting, and the only advice I got was from Lemon and Walder. On each patrol Captain Bath led us over the lines to fly up and down two or three miles on the German side of the trenches between the Scarpe and Armentières.

Our work consisted of: *line patrols* on which we flew between Armentières and the Scarpe to prevent any hostile machines from molesting our artillery observation aircraft or balloons; *offensive patrols* (O.P.s) on which we carried out attacks on the German observation machines and fighters with occasional sallies on to balloons, these latter being flown at five or six thousand feet and situated four or five miles on the German side of the lines; and *escorts*, when we accompanied two-seater machines of other squadrons to protect them from enemy attacks while carrying out bombing raids or photographic reconnaissance.

On patrols I had time to examine the country properly.

Lens, previously a mining and manufacturing town, was about two miles on the German side of the lines, immediately opposite us, and, as it was the most convenient landmark, we regarded it as the centre of our front. Seven or eight miles north of Lens was another small town, La Bassée, from which a long straight canal stretched across the lines to Bethune, the latter only seven miles from the trenches. To the northeast of Lens was the city of Lille, several miles on the German side of the line, while nearly opposite it, on our side, was the shattered town of Armentières. Directly north of this, also on the British side of the dividing line, the remains of Ypres formed the northernmost limit of our patrols.

To the south of Lens were Arras and Douai, the former being five miles on our side of the trenches occupied at that time and the latter, Douai, on the German side being more to the south-east and twelve miles from the line. The (land between these towns was a wilderness of shell-pocked, raw soil that stretched for several miles on both sides of the well-defined trenches. In the spring of 1917 the Canadian troops had effectively carried out the famous attack on Vimy Ridge and, pressing forward from some distance west of Souchez to take up a final position east of Vimy itself, had left behind them the old front line and German support trenches which, with the intensive shelling that had taken place, had converted the once rural scenery into an indescribable shambles. Between the La Bassée canal and the River Scarpe flowing between Arras and Douai there were no definite landmarks, the ground had taken on a uniform appearance which, from the air, looked as if both a steam roller and a plough had wrecked their worst efforts on it. To the south of the Scarpe this broadened out into the still greater desolation near Bapaume and Peronne.

On the north side of the La Bassée canal, however, there was one section of the line that puzzled every newcomer. It extended almost up to Armentières, an uneven front line and support trenches which in places were hardly visible. Everything was overgrown with grass and there was little sign that fighting was going on, or had taken place, there. We always referred to it as the 'Sector where the green grass grew all round!' It was occupied by the Portuguese, and as there did not seem to be any particular antipathy between the troops on either side of that sector, they let the grass grow over the trenches, the Germans saving their shells for more aggressive enemies to the north and south.

A few evenings after my arrival, Captain Bath, leading us on a patrol between Lens and Lille, got into a 'scrap' with some enemy fighters, and I had another disconcerting disillusionment about my capabilities as a fighter pilot. After seeing Bath 'wagging' his wings to signify that enemy machines were near, the whole of the flight commenced to stunt and to whirl about in a most disconcerting way. I did not see much of the fight, which proved to have been a veritable 'dog-fight' for, except that the surrounding air seemed to be full of zooming, turning, and diving machines, I did not recognise more than one of these as German.

Fortunately for me I had not caught the attention of any of the enemy, and after examining my Nieuport Captain Bath declared that I was a 'stout fellow'. I had stuck in a scrap and had not even a bullet hole in my machine. This unmerited praise made me all the more conscious of my unpreparedness for aerial fighting. To have been in a fight without having been able to discriminate between friend and enemy struck me as being the most dangerous form of stupidity. There had been seven German machines in the scrap and I had seen only one.

It was unfortunate for me that I did not confide my worry to Mannock, for several weeks later he told me that he had had similar experiences, and that by the time I joined the Squadron he had passed that stage in his development.

In this haphazard schooling our knowledge of actual war fighting was tempered on the hard anvil of experience. We won each item of wisdom only at the risk of our lives. The fault did not lie so much in the actual flying training as in the lack of instruction in the 'psychology of fighting'. Nothing had been done to 'key' me up to the dangers that assailed us.

One typical case occurred soon after my joining the flight. A new pilot arrived, and on his first patrol Captain Bath asked me to 'look after' him and to see that he did not get lost or otherwise leave the formation.

As soon as we were over the line and the enemy anti-aircraft gunners had got our range it was apparent that the newcomer was going to give us some trouble. Disliking the continuance of the shell bursts he flew off to the east and took up a course parallel to ours but about half a mile away. I also turned away from the flight in an attempt to encourage him to come back but, on seeing me approaching, he flew still farther east. After making two essays to get near him, finding myself about two miles from the flight, I turned back and fell into formation. The new 'bird' followed me back part of the way and resumed his first position to the east of our beat.

There was grave danger that a German flight might attack him, and as he was probably failing to keep a 'look-out', I anxiously scanned the sky behind us. Fortunately for him there were no enemy machines in our neighbourhood and when the patrol time was up, fearing he might not see us departing, I slinked towards him, wading through all the Archie bursts that had been intended for the flight. He was still stubborn and, in desperation, seeing him flying farther and farther east, I rolled my machine two or three times and then dived westward towards Bethune.

At last he realised that we were going home and, to my joy, I saw him following me.

With my little experience I had been anxious, but judging by what Captain Bath and the others had to say to him, my fears had been as nothing to theirs.

His only reply was to say that, as the flight seemed to *relish* flying where the shells were exploding, he did not see that he should be compelled to do so. Nothing we could say about the danger of his being attacked would persuade him that it was not only his duty to stay in the formation but, for his own safety, he must remain with the flight.

Whether he was conceited, stupid, or merely 'cussed', we never found out, for in the next fight in which we were engaged he remained 'outside' and we saw him no more. No one regretted his going, for in our vernacular 'he asked for it and got it'.

CHAPTER III

DURING my first two weeks with the Squadron there seemed to be a considerable number of departures and arrivals. Several pilots, amongst whom was Captain Allcock, were 'missing' and several others were posted to 'Home Establishment' after having served over six months with the Squadron. In the British attack on Vimy Ridge the casualties in our R.F.C. had been particularly heavy and pilots who had been through that strenuous time were tired and nerve-racked. To allow them time to recuperate, it was the custom to return them to England to act as instructors or to take up night flying in defence of London and the important towns. After three or four months of that they could expect to return to France, either to the same or to a different fighter squadron.

During the battle of Arras, in April 1917, the Nieuport was the premier fighter on our side. Its armament consisted of a single Lewis gun mounted on the top plane in such a way that it fired *above* the blades of the propeller, thus making the pilot fire fifteen degrees above his line of flight. When attacking an enemy machine from above, the Nieuport pilot had to dive at a much steeper angle than would a pilot who could fire along his line of flight with guns that were synchronised to fire between the blades of the propeller.

Opposed to the Nieuports were the German Albatros and Halberstadt fighters. These were faster than the Nieuport, carried two Spandau machine-guns which fired through the propeller, and could dive at between 200 and 225 m.p.h. With machines like these the Albatros or Halberstadt pilot could act according to his mood or his spirit. If he wanted to fight he could remain to do so, but if he thought that discretion was excusable he could avoid a combat either by flying straight or diving.

It also meant that the unfortunate Nieuport pilot, when the enemy cared to 'face' him, had to use every ounce of his flying and fighting ability to vanquish his adversary. When driven into a tight corner by superior numbers or by being taken at a serious tactical disadvantage, the Nieuport fighter had to depend entirely on his flying skill and determination.

The double-sized drums carried by the Lewis gun held ninety-six rounds of ammunition, and when a drum was exhausted the pilot had to fly his plane with his knees while using both hands to let down the gun and to change drums. The Germans on the other hand could fire five hundred rounds without releasing their firing levers. In both cases the guns were actually controlled by levers on the joy-stick.

Despite these advantages the enemy fighting planes had over the Nieuport, the latter was by no means obsolete, as I was later to find out. There was one asset that frequently was worth more than speed or guns — the spirit of the pilot. At that time and, in fact, throughout the war our fighter pilots waged an aggressive war, often many miles on the enemy's side of the trenches.

The Germans had fewer fighting machines than we and, either on account of this or because they lacked the truly aggressive spirit, their tactics were deficient in the confident abandon that appeals to the British. They always waited until their natural advantages placed us at their mercy before attacking us. Their only reason for entering into a combat was *Victory*, the destruction of our machines and our pilots. Whenever the 'game' was easy the enemy showed themselves to be capable and relentless antagonists. In addition there was the west wind, the prevailing wind in the north of France. It carried us quickly over the lines, but the time taken to traverse the same course on the return journey was frequently almost double the time. The anti-aircraft gunners had time to get our range correctly, and when in difficulties through engine failure, wounds, or other trouble, our chances of regaining the safety of our own lines were slight. My own experience, alone and with the flight, was that the farther the Germans were on their own side of the trenches the more aggressive they became, pressing home every advantage, both tactical and psychological. A pilot being attacked many miles over hostile country by an enemy flight was apt to suffer from that 'far from home' feeling that inspired Bairnsfather's famous war cartoon about 'Dirty work at the Cross-roads'.

My own most acute attack of this feeling took place about a fortnight after my arrival.

On two consecutive evening patrols the flight had attacked a German two-seater, a yellow camouflaged artillery co-operation machine that patrolled near Lille. On the evening following the second effort, the rhythm of 'Poet and Peasant' being played on the gramophone stirred me to activity. Sitting on the tennis court, ruminating on my inability either to 'spot' the enemy or to shoot at him when I did succeed in seeing him, the recollection of the yellow machine combined with the music imbued me with the determination to shoot it down.

I set off at once, and as I had expected, on approaching Lille amidst a cloud of Archie bursts, the sight of my *bête noir* flying an elliptical course north and south provided me with my first real 'thrill The sun was low on the horizon and the yellow and green markings showed up clearly from over a mile away. My head singing with hope and murder, I flew straight towards him; with the expression 'nasty stings in their rumps' ringing through my head. (The 'stings' were the observer's guns which could fire backwards.)

The Archie shelling stopped and the two-seater, instead of diving away as I had anticipated, only eased off a little to the east. I was at about eight thousand feet with the enemy about two thousand below my level and, diving on him with the wind whistling through the wiring and the le Rhone engine purring away easily, I pressed my eye to the Aldis sight. The yellow shape came properly into the lines and circles that enabled us to make allowances for the relative positions and speed of two machines and, breathlessly manoeuvring my Nieuport so that there should be no doubt that my bullets would hit the enemy, I pressed the firing lever.

Nothing happened, there was no clack-clacking of the gun; I had forgotten to 'cock' it. Being then within two hundred yards of the enemy I had perforce to pull out of the dive. As the gun was on the top plane the cocking lever was attached to a wire which hung down inside the windscreen alongside the wire which liberated the front of the gun to allow it to be lowered for reloading. In my anxiety and haste I pulled the wrong one, and the heavy weight of the Lewis gun hit me a stunning blow on the top of the head. Possibly the thickness of my flying helmet prevented a complete 'knock-out'. As it was, I was blinded and almost senseless when the pop-pop-pop of several machine-guns sounded from above. Hardly conscious of what was happening I threw my machine into a spin, round and round.

Urged on by the machine-gun fire, my wits returned quickly, and to my amazement and horror I saw six or seven machines circling round me and taking turns at firing at my spinning Nieuport.

It was then that 'lonely cross-roads' feeling assailed me. My machine was seven or eight miles from the lines, I was dazed and almost sick both with shock and fright, and the machine kept on spinning.

Seeing no end for me but a sanguinary mess on the ground if I continued, I pulled out of the spin at two thousand feet, to be met with a veritable cloud of smoke streamers from the enemy's explosive bullets. The trails shot past to the right and to the left and, amazed that none of them had hit me, I began to fly 'crazily', hoping that none of them would find their mark.

As I dived, sideslipped, half-rolled and threw the Nieuport about as if I were trying to break her in an attempt to avoid the terror of a 'flaming' end, the Germans attacked me with all the vigour of a pack of hounds after a defenceless stag.

The vivid sunset in the west threw up the darkness of the ground into sharp relief and, twisting and turning towards the distant safety of our lines to the accompaniment of the pop-pop-pop and poppety-pop of the German machine-guns, an overwhelming feeling of pathos and self-pity overcame me. I felt as if I wanted to dive straight into the ground — to finish it all.

This was fortunately a transient emotion and in a few seconds, glancing back at the faster machines behind me that seemed so intent on committing coldblooded murder, I began to swear and curse everything from my own stupidity to the Kaiser.

On one of the turns I succeeded in loading the gun. My spirits had returned to such an extent that I was considering rounding on the Germans to curse them with bullets when another horror awoke me. The enemy anti-aircraft gunners, fearing that I was going to escape, simultaneously decided to fire every available gun directly ahead of me. There must have been at least twenty bursts within a hundred and fifty yards of my machine; not the small bursts to which we were accustomed when flying at over ten thousand feet, but heavy, nerve-shattering detonations that blasted every atom of courage from me. What had previously been a rout turned into a complete and stomach-shaking panic, driving me to even more frantic evolutions to escape.

At that time it seemed to me inconceivable that the Nieuport could exist amongst the shell bursts, or that the engine, the tank, and I myself could escape the bullets; but luck was on my side and, having kept persistently moving towards the sunset that had smiled so ironically on my flight, the cessation of the shelling came as a surprise to me.

On our side of the line all was peace — the air to the east was a mass of heavy black shell bursts. With trembling hands and throbbing head, I pushed the Lewis gun back on to its mounting.

I was quite unconscious of having breathed during the whole debacle and, flying over the now darkening trenches, my breath came in heavy sighs as the clear fresh air went deep into my lungs. My relief at having escaped unhurt quickly gave way to anger, the anger of a puppy that realises it has been teased — that it has shown fear of something of which it has no right to be afraid. To prove to the enemy that I was not exactly suffering from a 'blue funk', a childish, puppy-dog thought, I climbed to five thousand feet and recrossed the lines. This time, as there were no enemy machines in sight, the Archie gunners having already wasted so much ammunition on me fired at me only in a desultory way as I flew southwards towards Lens and 'Home'.

Possibly because the souvenirs my machine had to show for what to me had been a nerve-racking ordeal were but a few scattered bullet holes, the same panic never again gripped me. It taught me several lessons, however. The two-seater pilot, having been attacked twice by the same flight at the same hour of the day, had evidently arranged to act as a 'decoy'. In my haste to come to grips with him I had not even thought of the possibility of other hostile machines being in the neighbourhood. I had attacked with enough spirit, but had failed to make the elementary preparation of loading my gun. I had lost my head completely and had mistaken the release wire for the loading wire.

Determined that these defects in my training would have to be remedied, the next afternoon I went up on an 'educational' flight to practise handling my gun and to accustom myself to 'spotting' machines.

On the way to the lines I meditated on the methods adopted by the pilots of the Fokker machines in climbing to a great height and then diving straight down on to their victims much in the manner of a hawk. Deciding to emulate them I climbed steadily towards Arras and then, turning east, practised letting down my gun, replacing it and firing short bursts of four or five rounds. My altimeter read 16,000 feet as, still climbing, I crossed the lines towards Douai.

After a minute or two the anti-aircraft gunners got my range and the shells came up in bursts of four. The first lot exploded a little to the left and above me, but the second was immediately ahead, the nearest burst being only about fifty or sixty feet away. Somehow this did not worry me and, remembering Captain Bath's tactics under these circumstances, I moved to the right for two or three hundred yards before turning again to the east. The third group exploded to my left and a little ahead of me — in the position I should have been had I kept on the same line of flight. By continuing this manoeuvre I succeeded in keeping at a safe distance from the bursts until the gunner, getting tired of firing shells into 'thin air', gave up the attempt to hit me or even to harass me.

My experience the previous evening had taught me to suspect any cessation of hostilities on the part of the gunners and, while still continuing to fly an erratic course, I scanned the sky all round me, particularly above and to the south-west where the sun made it impossible to see anything. In the crystal-clear air at that height the sunlight virtually made one 'blind' on the sunny side and, dreading that some 'Fokker' or Albatros might be sitting up there waiting for me, I flew first to one side then the other, essaying to see anything that might be hidden in the glare.

Having reassured myself on this score I searched underneath me for a potential victim, but as far as I could see there was no machine in sight, either friendly or hostile. I spent a quarter of an hour fooling about like this, circling over Douai, dodging the few small anti-aircraft shells, and practising all sorts of manoeuvres. Then, two black dots that appeared to the north-west gradually resolved themselves into aeroplanes. They were a few hundred feet above my level and were evidently hostile. Climbing to meet them I realised that the 'lines' were ten or twelve miles away. The 'dirty work' feeling again came into my mind; but this time I was prepared, I had sufficient height to be clear of dangerous Archie, and there were only two opponents.

As they dived, a hundred yards apart, I swung round to the left, hoping that by so doing I would have to face only one at a time. Both of them fired bursts in my direction, but the smoke streamers were fifteen or twenty feet to the right of my machine and on turning round at right angles to this course I flew underneath the nearest one and got a good sight on the second. The latter was pulling up, preparatory to turning, when I pressed the firing lever and heard the cheery 'clacky-clacky' of my Lewis gun. The tracer ammunition went straight into the fuselage just behind the engine. The German was only a hundred yards away and the helmeted head of the observer was clearly visible in my sight — but he was not looking in my direction. I was wondering if my bullets had killed the pilot, when the sound of the other one's gun recalled my attention to *him*. Circling round suddenly, I caught sight of a dark machine with a pointed nose flying off to the north. The first machine by this time was diving at an increasingly steep angle and I was confident I had obtained my 'first' victory.

With the realisation that I had been 'blooded' I flew back towards the lines to the accompaniment of the angry barks of the anti-aircraft shells. Approaching the trenches in a long steady dive, my ear drums were nearly shattered by one of the worst explosions I had ever heard. There was only one, and although it was quite two hundred yards from me the detonation made my Nieuport quiver and my heart thump.

On returning, I reported the scrap, but as I had been so far on the enemy side of the lines no one had even seen the machines. It appeared that lack of supporting evidence invalidated my claim. It was also pointed out to me by Major Tilney that only pilots who had 'Roving Commissions' were allowed to fly on the other side of the lines.

Nevertheless I felt that this exploit had established me with Godfrey, Bond, Hall and Keen, for the next afternoon Hall offered to accompany me on a similar flight. This time, despite a twenty minutes' patrol over and past Douai, we failed to find any enemy machines. On the return journey, losing height in preparation for attacking a two-seater which ultimately turned out to be one of our own R.E.8's, the 'heavy' Archie gunner found our range and his single shell exploded above us with a crashing roar.

Hall was a doughty scrapper, and the fact that he volunteered to cross the lines with me I regarded as a great compliment.

Every flight added its quota to my war education, revealing some new and unexpected feature, or making me better acquainted with those I already knew. How I envied fighters like Bond, Blaxland, Walder, Hall, Lemon, Godfrey, Keen and Redler! They were seasoned warriors. Both Bond and Godfrey had succeeded in bringing down two enemy machines in one day. They were my idols during those first weeks. Godfrey, 'Steve' as we knew him, had a 'Roving Commission' which meant that he could do exactly as he pleased, going up when he felt inclined and landing anywhere on the front. Steve was a Canadian whose speech was as trenchant as his fighting was aggressive, and his warlike Nieuport was fitted with a special gadget of his own to carry a double Lewis gun.

Hall and Redler were South Africans, English South Africans with all the colonial determination and level-headedness. Bond was English, a correspondent of one of the daily papers. He spent a good deal of his time writing, and there was frequently a good deal of discussion between him and the C.O. as to what would pass the censor. He was about five feet seven or eight, had a cheery smile, and did everything with an unassuming air that increased everyone's admiration. He had the M.C. and bar.

During my first fortnight with the squadron my chief interests were: learning the habits of the 'line' and discussions with Mannock. The latter was unfit for flying for several days through getting a small piece of steel into his eye. He became morbid and, mooning round the camp like a bandaged buccaneer, he presented a picture of dejection and misery. On hearing of my scrap near Douai he seemed pleased. "That's the only way to learn, but it's no use putting in a claim unless you are immediately over the trenches. The best way to get confirmation is to bring 'em down as corpses on this side."

He seemed very worried, and before his eye was better his turn for leave arrived.

In the middle of June two pilots who had learnt to fly with me were posted to the Squadron, G. B. Crole and Peter Wylie Smith. Crole was an Oxford 'Double Blue', also Scotch, and 'Peter Wylie' as Smith was known, hailed from Australia. Both were good fellows, and Crole, popularly known as 'Gerry', having served previously as an observer, quickly fitted into the life of the Squadron. His first solo on a Nieuport was a glaring example of the dangers of sending a new pilot up in a 'difficult' machine.

This particular Nieuport required not only full left rudder, but one had to *kick the rudder hard over* as she touched the ground. Crole had never conceived the possibility of 'kicking' a rudder bar quite so hard as this one required and, despite my warning, the machine turned a complete Catherine wheel immediately on touching the ground. Major Tilney and I, followed by the mechanics, sprinted out to the wreck to drag Crole from the overturned fuselage. He was badly shaken and had a bruised leg, but was otherwise unhurt.

Rugger Blues have to be capable of withstanding a good deal of battering without flinching, and despite his injured leg and the shaking Crole went up in a better machine, this time making a perfect landing.

Peter Wylie, on the other hand, never quite succeeded in mastering the Nieuport. He could land fairly well, but in the air the idiosyncrasies of the machine caused him endless trouble; so much so that, despite his willingness to go on trying and his undoubted courage, Major Tilney was at last forced to send him to Candas for 'Further Instruction'.

My short experience had impressed on me the necessity for a pilot having complete control over his machine, and when I explained this to P.W. it softened the blow. He was determined to come back to the Squadron and, after a fortnight's experience on Nieuports, he achieved his ambition in returning to us.

Meanwhile, my own education was progressing and, taking the advice Mick had given me, I spent a good part of the day when I was not on an official patrol with the flight, in chasing up and down the line, frequently making excursions as far as Douai and Henin Lietard. On one such trip, returning towards Arras from south of Douai I was crossing the lines at twelve thousand feet when I caught a glimpse of a dark red and black machine fourteen or fifteen hundred feet below me. There was a thin filmy layer of cloud which periodically obscured my view, but I succeeded in following the German until I could recognise the markings on his top plane. It was an Albatros, red and black, and as I drew up behind it, taking careful aim and holding my fire until within point-blank range, the pilot was looking over the side towards the line, probably searching for an R.E.8 or A.W.[1]

---

[1] Artillery observation machines.

I fired about twenty rounds. The Albatros put its nose up into the air, rearing like a wounded animal, high up in front of me. Then it fell over. With grim curiosity I watched, waiting to get another sight on it in case the pilot were shamming. But it was only too true, flames began licking round the fuselage, and as the machine dived I saw the flame getting larger and longer. A cloud of black smoke belched out of the fuselage and I knew then that the deadly work was done.

It was the first time I had ever seen a machine in flames. Horrified and soul-sickened at having sent a human being, even an enemy, to such a miserable death, I flew away from the spot as quickly as possible — away to the north, towards Lens, never daring to look backwards.

It was a long time before I ventured to land, and when I did the thought of sending in a 'claim' for it was so abhorrent that I contented myself with saying that I had fired at an E.A. (Enemy Aircraft). Besides I was afraid of what might be said of me for using ammunition which could set a machine on fire. The burning machine fell on our side of the lines and, as it happened that I had been the only fighter in the air at the time, ironically enough for me, the burnt remains were brought to 'A' flight. By the time these arrived my feeling of nausea had worn off. I had persuaded myself that my first bullets had killed the pilot. The war-hardening influence was already at work.

Later on it was my misfortune to see several of our pilots crashing down to a flaming end, the machine diving ahead of its comet-like tail of black smoke and flames. Thenceforward I came to regard the vision of a flaming enemy without a tremor — but with an inward prayer that the pilot had been killed first. When a tank is punctured the leaking petrol flows over the pilot's legs and body and the next tracer or explosive bullet sets it alight — a horrible thought, for even in a straight dive it took our machines nearly a minute to descend from sixteen thousand feet — a minute of agonising terrifying seconds, finishing in a cloud of smoke and flames on the ground after the engine had buried itself deep in the soft earth.

Besides the prospect of such an end ahead of us, for it was always a menace because of the presence of tracer and explosive ammunition, we were faced with the dangers of forced landings, bad landings or mechanical trouble, which could result in serious injury or even death. Many times pilots crashed on returning from patrol, the tyres on their landing wheels having been punctured by bullets or Archie splinters. Engine failure above or on the other side of the lines usually meant that the machine had to descend amongst trenches, shell-holes, barbed wire or ruins. Crashes of this type were almost a daily occurrence and yet very few pilots were killed.

A nasty one fell to my lot, nasty because it possibly did more to shake my confidence in my flying ability than anything had done, but it taught me a severe lesson — that, during the whole time in the air, a pilot must never relax.

One Sunday morning, while descending to land on the aerodrome I heard a grinding crash, after which I could not remember anything until, with a glorious feeling of lightness and unreality, a vision of a 'Kaloma' in white appeared straight ahead of me. ('Kaloma' was the name given to a popular print of a beautiful and seductive woman.)

'Kaloma' in white gradually became more and more real, and ultimately turned out to be a nurse looking down on me from the foot of a bed in the Bruay Casualty Clearing Station, No. 22 C.C.S.

I never succeeded in elucidating the details of the accident beyond the bare statement that I had crashed into another machine. Whatever had happened, it proved to me that one could be flying quite serenely one minute, and, as far as consciousness was concerned, find oneself lying in hospital the next. Apart from concussion my only apparent injuries were cuts and bruises.

During the following days I was confined to bed, and Major Tilney, Walder and Steve Godfrey paid me frequent visits. Steve broke the news to me that if I were more than five days away from the Squadron the C.O. would have to strike me off the strength.

I hated the thought of having to leave the Squadron, and on the Friday, when the Matron came to me to ask if I wanted to be sent to the Duchess of Westminster's Hospital at the base, I became alarmed. She told me the whole hospital had to be cleared to make room for the anticipated casualties resulting from an attack that was to take place that day. The Base Hospital spelt 'Blighty' to the unfortunates who *were* wounded, but as I considered there was nothing much wrong with me and that it would take me only another day or two to recover, I opposed the suggestion wholeheartedly. The doctor's decision that I was too ill to be moved anyway settled the matter for the time being.

In the evening Major Tilney came to enquire if there were any hope of my returning to the Squadron, and later Mannock arrived. He had just returned from leave and, sitting by my bed in the ward full of empty expectant beds, his vigour and mental alertness combined with his healthy ruggedness drove home to me my own weakness. He sat talking for over an hour.

His eye was better and his mental attitude had undergone a complete change. He no longer girded at circumstances or railed at snobbery. His moroseness had given way to excitement and optimism.

He talked eagerly of the power that each man has within himself, the power which will enable him to override circumstances. His rest in England had given him time to appreciate my side of the argument; the social equality of all men in personal and National emergencies. Having found a new strength in this he declaimed all the more bitterly against the empty Jingoism that was rampant in England; against those who were exploiting the Nation's misfortune for their own financial or ambitious ends.

"But that has nothing to do with us out here," he said. "We've got to get on with the work and leave the retribution until afterwards. *Fellows like ourselves who understand what we are doing have got to put every ounce into it.*"

I had been puzzled by his frequent attacks on 'snobbery'. He had shown none of the usual signs of class consciousness, but as he continued to talk, eloquently, I began to see his point of view.

After spending a year in a prisoners' camp in Turkey, he had returned to England filled with his own idealistic brand of patriotism. Believing that everyone would be doing his best to fight for the country, he had expected to find that those whom he had been taught to respect would be in the vanguard of the fighting forces. Instead, he had discovered that the energy fellows put into fighting for their country was frequently inversely proportionate to the amenities and social privileges they enjoyed. The supposed 'pride' in family, school, university, and nationality of hundreds had been exposed as worthless by fellows who used their social positions to obtain comfortable service jobs at home or safe billets behind the lines overseas. As with all of us, anyone who 'pulled his full weight' in the fighting commanded Mick's admiration, irrespective of rank or position.

The angelic personification of 'Kaloma', the ward sister, brought us some tea and told Mick that after it was finished he had better depart.

Mick looked at her, quizzically, admiring her gentle features and seductive expression, then turning to me said:

"Look here, you old blighter, I know why you like lying here. I'll have to see about having a spell in hospital myself."

When Mannock left there was an air of quiet preparedness about the hospital, the ambulances had gone up the line and the dressers' trolleys were standing in the middle of the ward, laden with bandages, instruments and antiseptic lotions. The sister came in several times to see that everything was in order. Poor girl, she knew what was ahead of her. I didn't.

At nine o'clock the first ambulances arrived, and stretcher after stretcher was carried in, each containing its torn and battered sample of war's brutality. These were the worst cases, the desperately wounded who required immediate attention, amputations mostly, but several with internal bullet and shrapnel wounds. The smell of wounds and antiseptic was mixed with the stench of unwashed feet, but the sister, her face paler and her lips pressed tight to keep them from trembling, went from one to the other, giving an injection here and arranging a bandage there.

Several of the fellows, Canadians, were moaning and, as I had some experience of surgery, I got up and offered to help.

"You go back to bed," Sister said forcefully. "There are enough orderlies here."

Something in my bearing must have worried her, for soon afterwards, finding me sitting up in bed looking round the ward anxiously, she brought me a cup of tea and said laconically, "You'll sleep after that."

The horrible liquid must have been drugged for, when I awoke, daylight was streaming in through the windows.

Every bed was occupied. The sister had disappeared and two orderlies were lifting a wounded fellow into the end bed. He had just returned from the operating theatre and was still unconscious.

In the bed on my right was a youngster, crying and swearing alternately.

"Got a gasper, bo'?" he asked. As I handed him one and lit it for him he indicated the fellow on the next bed with his thumb.

"God — have you seen *him*?"

I saw only the bedclothes with a ball of bandages through which the blood was oozing insistently.

"No — what's wrong?" I asked.

The young Canadian was almost hysterical about it. "He hasn't any bloody face at all."

His crying had been for those around him, not because of the bullet that was in his own stomach.

For an hour or two I assisted the orderlies. Action was better than lying still and being once more on my feet, I quickly determined to get out of it as soon as possible. The doctors and the qualified nurses were in the operating theatre where they had been working without a break through the whole night. There was no one to prevent my leaving the hospital and, about one o'clock, carefully taking my card from above my bed, I told one of the orderlies that the bed was 'vacated'.

On the way to the aerodrome I had a drink of champagne and brandy at the estaminet, and when I ultimately reached 'A' flight's hangar my whole scheme had evolved. If I could manage to put in a flight to prove that I was again fit for flying I could get my official discharge from hospital.

The mechanics were surprised to see me and, because they knew that I had been 'struck off the strength', the flight sergeant refused to let me have my own Nieuport.

"I'd better ask the C.O. first," Sergeant Thompson said, and hurried off to the orderly room.

He returned, accompanied by Major Tilney who, seeing the bandages still on my head, remarked: "Good Heavens, Mac, you're not fit for flying! You're as white as a sheet."

However, Major Tilney was a sport, and on hearing my scheme he agreed to let me take a machine up, on my own responsibility. If anything serious happened I was to say that I had gone up without permission.

In the air I felt very 'shaky', but succeeded in landing with only a broken tail skid.

After that everything was easy. The tired doctors and nurses at the hospital were too busy to attend to small matters like 'runaway' patients. I was able to pack my few belongings and return to camp without hindrance.

CHAPTER IV

WHETHER because of my talk with Mannock the previous evening, or because of the shock of seeing the war-wounded in the hospital, or because of my own physical weakness, my outlook on life and fighting became more subdued. Instead of floundering about in a sea of reckless optimism as the result of my ignorance of the terrible facts of war, I found a refuge in the fatalism of all those who were daily risking their lives for the country. The nation came first — individual suffering last. I wanted to probe deeper into the general principles, to understand the ethics of and the methods of waging a war.

Previously I had formed but a hazy idea of my surroundings, the camp and the battlefields. Now I began to take an interest in them. As my nerves were still uncertain and every second flight necessitated the fitting of a new tail skid and sometimes a complete lower wing, I took Major Tilney's advice and, when not on official patrol, spent a good deal of my time visiting neighbouring towns and hunting for friends. By the C.O.'s indulgence I was allowed a motorcycle and side-car to take me as far away as Bapaume so that I might visit a school-friend; to Arras, Doullens or even 'up the line', where one or two friends were fighting. On one of these trips another unpleasant shock awaited me.

I managed to locate a school-friend and, filled with the hope that I would find him out of the line on 'rest' and that we would be able to join in a 'Binge' in Bethune, I drove off towards the trenches. On reaching his company I was told that he was in the Casualty Clearing Station, and when I enquired for him there the doctor told me that he had died of bullet wounds the previous day.

Other trips I made were to neighbouring squadrons where I usually found friends with whom I had learnt to fly, and the details of their work assisted me in developing a much wider outlook on the war that was constantly being waged in the air.

Nearest us was No. 2 Squadron at Hesdigneul on the Bethune road. The machines were heavy Armstrong Whitworth two-seaters, known as A.W.s, and their principal duty consisted of artillery co-operation on which they flew over the trenches at anything from two thousand feet to six thousand feet, depending on the visibility and the location of the target. More dangerous work was demanded of them for low bombing attacks on rail-heads and supply columns as well as photographic reconnaissance for intelligence purposes. We frequently saw them miles on the German side of the line, surrounded by clouds of Archie bursts, plodding at their disagreeable tasks. When their duties were likely to engage them for a sufficiently long time to allow German fighters to take off to attack, we of '40' had to provide an escort, whose special duty it was to prevent the enemy fighters from 'molesting' the cumbersome two-seaters.

At Auchel, only three miles away, were Nos. 25 and 43. '25' was principally a bombing squadron equipped with large pusher type F.E.2D.s in which the observer was in front of the pilot and, with his machine-gun, could 'rake' everything in front or above the F.E. They also carried out artillery observation and photographic work. At night we often heard them passing over Bruay on their way to bomb German aerodromes and towns on the German side. We occasionally had to escort them on daylight bombing raids on Valenciennes and neighbouring railways.

'43' was a different type of squadron altogether. Their machines were Sopwith two-seaters, the famous 'one-and-a-half-strutters' that had done such noble work in wresting the supremacy from the Fokker in 1916. They were essentially fighting machines, but because they carried observers and in 1917 were almost obsolete on account of their lack of speed (80-90 m.p.h.) they performed many daring feats in obtaining photographs of strategic points that were urgently required.

The remaining two squadrons with which we came in close contact were No. 8, a Naval (R.N.A.S.) Squadron stationed at Mont St. Eloi and flying single-seater fighters, Sopwith Triplanes. They operated on our front, and their patrols were arranged to dovetail with ours. The Triplane was faster than the Nieuport, and near the ground could manoeuvre better, a fact which never failed to annoy Barlow. The other was No. 16, a Canadian Squadron of R.E.S's, whose almost sole duty was artillery co-operation. On every flight over the lines we met their ugly two-seaters dodging Archie while the observers sent down their wireless messages to the batteries with which they were working. The pride of the senior pilots in No. 16 was that they never 'gave-way' to the German fighters unless they were hopelessly outnumbered, but, staying to fight, succeeded occasionally in bringing down enemy fighters.

Between these squadrons and ourselves the spirit of camaraderie was cemented by the kindly link, our beloved Padre Keymer.

Everything that happened at that time seemed to be driving the spirit of war deeper into me, making me all the more determined to wage a personal as well as a national war against the enemy. The national spirit predominated when we were on patrol or when chasing enemy two-seaters away from the lines; but whenever I succeeded in getting my machine within range of the enemy it became a war of personal enmity.

Although all the others were probably conscious of these feelings our lives were not altogether filled by the war. Tennis, cards, music on the gramophone, dinners in Bethune, Amiens, or occasionally St. Omer, provided sufficient relaxation into which everyone entered with gusto. Living for the day as we were, it mattered little what we did; our situation allowed us to forget the war and share the pleasures of the non-combatant forces behind the lines. This appealed to me as the most comfortable method of waging war. We had exceedingly cosy quarters, a respectable mess, a tennis court, and, when we felt inclined, could dine at a proper hotel. Yet, with all this in our favour, the risks run by fighter pilots were probably greater than those any other troops had to face. Our 'expectation of life' was journalistically computed at *three weeks*.

In the evenings it was our custom to sit round the tennis court listening to the gramophone and arguing about theatres, sport and the war.

Amongst the pilots that had been posted to the Squadron, besides Crole and P. W. Smith, was Davis, a tall, heavily built Englishman with fair hair. He was a keen sportsman and, much to 'A' flight's relief, proved to be a capable pilot as well as a stout fellow. In his first scraps he managed to do better than the majority of us had done.

Almost imperceptibly the Squadron changed. Pilots were with us one day and the next night a new pilot would be sitting at the foot of the table. Another arrival was a Flight Commander, 'Zulu' Lloyd. He had served with No. 60, one of our sister 'Nieuport' squadrons; and as Bond, Mannock, Godfrey, Redler, Hall, Lemon and the other scrappers were anxious to hear what methods, if any, were adopted by '60', they held dining-table conferences on tactics. To my great astonishment and delight I was invited to take part in these.

'Zulu' was a South African as were Hall, Redler and Tudhope. He possessed a charming manner, a sort of boyish ingenuousness that disarmed any criticism or animosity. He had been given command of a flight in a squadron which should have been able to produce its own commanders. Despite any jealousy which might otherwise have existed, the round, cheery-faced South African immediately won the confidence of the whole Squadron.

There was a strong undercurrent of dissension in the Squadron during July — not levelled at Zulu, but against Mannock. Somehow several of the others noted the change that had taken place in him. He was no longer silent while they talked, his sense of social inferiority had vanished, but he found himself face to face with a new kind of snobbery, that of fighting prowess. He had been three months with the Squadron and had only brought down two enemy machines. One or two pilots even declared that Mick had 'stayed out' when the others went into scraps. They resented the development of his self-assurance and optimism.

Poor Mick! His 'assurance' was but the fruit of his idealism and hope. As he had never discussed his fighting experiences with me I could not estimate the justice of the aspersions that were thrown at him.

To stay out of a scrap was regarded as 'cowardice' (a capital crime in the infantry), and those who did so were rarely allowed to take part in conversations about the war. The Squadron showed no mercy to the quitter, and feeling was so high that I was once taken to task by Steve Godfrey and Hall for having walked to Bruay to take a drink with a pilot they regarded as belonging to this category. They declared that no matter what his school might have been he was no fit companion for me. As I was almost untried at the time I thought this either a subtle piece of flattery or the result of vindictiveness; but later it transpired that they had good reason. It was a notorious fact that 'quitting' was infectious, that where one fellow failed, his friend, even in a different flight, was liable to fail too.

Had it not been for Mannock and the fact that I had already been accepted as a 'stout fellow', one morning I might easily have found myself amongst the 'quitters'. It happened very simply.

Captain Bath, leading the flight, dived on seven or eight Germans near Henin Lietard. It was obviously going to be a desperate fight, for the Germans rounded on us, and as we dived in amongst them I looked about, trying to distinguish friend from enemy. The air became full of stunting, scrapping machines. Here and there were the flashes of British tracer bullets or the smoke trails of the Germans'. I was able to distinguish several of the enemy and, getting my sight on one of them, pressed my firing lever. The gun had been cocked, but it refused to fire more than two rounds. I tried the cocking wire only to find that the gun had jammed properly. The fight was going on all round me and, remembering Steve Godfrey's advice, I quickly threw the machine into a spin, holding the joy-stick back between my legs, while letting down the gun.

Luckily the Germans were being too closely engaged by the remainder of the flight to notice my predicament, and while spinning down to two or three thousand feet I succeeded in dismantling the Lewis. It was a hopeless effort, however, the chrome nickel steel bolt had broken right through.

Glancing hurriedly round to make sure that none of the enemy had followed me down, I pulled out of the spin.

The flight was in the distance, receiving the attentions of Archie, and even above the roar of my engine the dull thuds of the explosions were clearly audible. It was obviously futile for me to attempt to rejoin them, so I climbed steadily towards the Scarpe and the far-off trenches. The gun, hanging down from its pillar with the mechanism lying on my lap, appeared to me the last word in inefficiency. The hard shining steel bolt over an inch in thickness was broken — leaving me at the absolute mercy of any stray German machine that happened to see me. I might as well have been a civilian.

Putting the two pieces of the bolt into my pocket I reassembled the remainder and pushed the gun back on to its mounting. If I were unarmed I could at least appear to be warlike and, seeing the amusing as well as the dangerous side of the situation, I 'stunted' my way over the trenches at three thousand feet, the Archie hounds yapping in full cry behind me.

My reception at the Squadron was far from amusing. Major Tilney, Mannock and one or two others came out to demand the reason for my leaving the flight in the middle of a patrol.

My explanation did not seem to them satisfactory, particularly when they heard there had been a scrap, and it was only when the armourer discovered that there was no bolt in the gun that the tension eased at all.

I showed them the broken pieces, but even that did not acquit me. There was the bald fact, I had left the flight in the middle of a scrap, and when Captain Bath and the remainder returned it appeared as if I was going to have a hard time.

Mick, however, had been thinking, and, raising his voice, said: "Do you know that he had the guts to dismantle his Lewis in a scrap. He came back here with a broken bolt in his pocket and his gun reassembled. If any of you has either the ability or the courage to do that you're a damned sight better than I think you are."

Mick was really angry. The occasion had given him an opportunity 'to let off steam' and as, in addition, Steve

Godfrey showed some interest in how I had managed to dismantle the gun while spinning, my name was cleared. I was still a stout fellow.

Mannock's attitude was very typical of him, for on one occasion when his own gun jammed in a scrap he had carried on with the flight armed only with a Very Pistol. I had not even had that.

Although there were mutterings about one or two of the pilots, somehow the gradual changing of the personnel seemed to remedy matters. Many new pilots arrived after me, promising 'stout fellows': Crole, Tudhope, Pettigrew, Kennedy, Rook, P. W. Smith, Harrison, Herbert. Herbert was a sergeant pilot, a fact which we all resented so much that Major Tilney recommended him for a commission at a later date.

Harrison and Kennedy, both Canadians, were posted to 'A' flight. Harrison was an enigma to the rest of us. He was about six feet tall, rather swarthy, and as his bristly hair, which defied all attempts at brushing, stood straight up from his head, his appearance was that of a quarrelsome backwoodsman. We did not immediately accept 'Harrie' as one of us. He had his own ideas about the war and about the flight, the expression of which ideas frequently got him into trouble. He neither smoked nor drank.

It fell to my lot to take him up on his first instructional flight over the lines. Harrie's case was rather typical during those rush months when fighter pilots were sent overseas with anything between twenty to fifty hours' flying to their credit. He had never flown in formation and had no conception of even flying in a straight line.

Having been told to fly as close to me as possible he did his best, his alarming best, for, failing to control either his forward speed or his direction, he would appear for a few seconds on my right, then, after getting behind me, would come up on my left in a series of jerks and sideslips.

At first I flew along steadily, hoping he would ultimately get control of his machine, but after he had dived in front of me, sideslipped over me so that his undercarriage wheel nearly hit my machine-gun, and had brought his top wing-tip almost within my grasp, I signed to him to keep at a safe distance. Even then his inability to fly straight caused his machine to vary its position relative to mine by anything up to a hundred yards in any of the three dimensions.

I kept him at it for two hours, chasing up and down immediately above the trenches, and as he showed some signs of improvement during the last half-hour, my anger was slightly appeased.

On landing I had my first taste of Harrie's tongue.

I was telling Bath and Redler about my escapes from death when Harrie joined us.

"Of all the bloody fool pilots I've met, this fellow takes the 'x-y-z' cake," he said, addressing Captain Bath.

The others might have been persuaded that I had been playing tricks with my pupil had not Harrie's first trip with the flight proved so disconcerting. It was well recognised that a flight commander should not 'look for trouble' with an entirely inexperienced pilot in the flight, but on this first patrol we did not have to look for it, we had all the trouble we needed in our midst; amongst us, above us, below us. Harrie's Nieuport seemed to bear a grudge against all the others; it would come charging sideways towards us and, on our making frantic efforts to avoid a collision, we would be greeted by the sight of Harrie careering off in an equally desperate sideslip towards the next machine.

When we landed, Captain Bath, knowing that only true backwood vernacular would have any effect, told Harrison what he thought of his exhibition. Harrie was quite unperturbed. His one explosive outburst was enough for Bath.

"Not one of you 'x-y-z's' can fly straight. I'll get the C.O. to put me into another flight."

Those of us who remained afterwards grew very fond of the tall, stubborn Harrie. When he learnt to keep formation we could rely on him to do anything required of him without turning one of his equally stubborn hairs. As with many of his type his aggressively taciturn manner failed to annoy us when we knew what he had in him.

Kennedy, on the other hand, was a genial antidote to Harrison. He had studied at Toronto University, was twenty-one, and a particularly keen sense of humour soon made him popular in the mess. Both Harrison and he were inveterate poker players,, and their advent made the poker-table the battlefront of the mess. A game between 'Steve' Godfrey, Harrison, 'George' Pettigrew, Kennedy and Hall always provided us with some amusement. Harrison, the inscrutable, only occasionally bluffed. Steve was always ready to 'put the other fellow up'; while 'George', eager and forceful, did his best to raise the pitch of the game if not the tempers of the players.

Rook was another Canadian, a charming boy whose negligee garb was a short red Oxford jacket. He was only nineteen, the same age as Barlow. These two, the babies of the Squadron, had much in common. Rook was always prepared for a quiet 'jape', and Barlow, with typical boisterous spirits, was ever ready to turn the jape into a 'rag The only difference between them was that Rook regarded the war with due seriousness while Barlow treated it as if it were really a 'rag' on a stupendous scale.

One morning Barlow, the irrepressible, gave us a fine example of his spirit. A pilot of No. 8 Naval Squadron, against whom Barlow seemed to bear a grudge, had 'raided' a German aerodrome and had claimed to have done considerable damage. The idea of attacking the Germans in their own aerodromes appealed to Barlow, so he set out to emulate the feat or to go one better. We never found out what he had really intended doing, for when he returned he was flushed and almost speechless with excitement. He had shot down a German machine but had been peppered all the way back to the lines. His machine had suffered both from bullets from the air and the ground, and as there could be no direct confirmation of his claim a short conference was held to consider whether or not his exploit was worthy of reporting.

This attitude towards an ingenuous and plucky youngster annoyed me. As I was one of the members of the 'conference' I soon realised the truth of what Mick had said about 'producing the corpse'. While there were undoubtedly many cases of false claims by unscrupulous pilots, the opinion of one's fellow-pilots could usually determine whether the claim was likely to be just or not. No one was despised more than the 'hot-air merchant' whose combat reports showed a vainglorious attempt at 'wish fulfilment'. Barlow was not one of this type.

These lone 'strafes' were a feature of the fighting on our front at that time and, although ours were carried out in a haphazard way and as the result of high spirits and aggressiveness because we were a 'fighter' squadron, the two-seater reconnaissance and bombing machines on each side occasionally managed to carry out what were probably better organised raids.

Early in July one of the large German two-seaters, finding the air clear of Nieuports, succeeded in penetrating on our side as far as our aerodrome. We watched the machine, almost invisible from the ground because of the brilliant sunbelt; and as he did not drop bombs we presumed he was carrying out a reconnaissance either of Army Headquarters at Hondain or more probably of the aerodromes at Auchel, Hesdigneul and Bruay. With supreme optimism Mick jumped into his machine to cut off the raider on his return to the line, but as the German was flying at eighteen or nineteen thousand feet, Mick's chances of catching him were very small. When the German disappeared in the distant east, Mick's machine had reached only ten thousand feet.

At night either the same or another German pilot came over again. We were playing poker in the mess and while we were waiting for Harrie to 'put Godfrey up' the deep throb of a heavy German engine drowned our voices. The machine passed over the camp and someone yelled: "Put your lights out."

I was about to extinguish the candles, but Harrison expostulated. "Here — wait till this game's finished, lie's after the aerodrome, not us."

In a few seconds the bombs began exploding, and on hurrying round to the hangars we found that three bombs had hit the aerodrome. Fortunately the holes, still reeking, were out in the middle of the field.

This attack was possibly the result of our bright aluminium planes showing up clearly on photographs the German had taken in the afternoon.

The raid had a decisive effect on Mannock. The next afternoon, while he and I were sitting in the rose bower of Odette's garden, demolishing the dainty cakes the little French girl had made for us, he suddenly slapped his forehead with the palm of his hand.

"I've got no right to be sitting here! I ought to be up there waiting for the next two-seater that comes over."

Odette understood his meaning and pretended to be annoyed.

"But Monsieur deserves the tea I have made for him. To-morrow I will allow you to go up and kill the Boche. You don't like to come here?"

Mick laughed at her.

"But will you say that to-night when they come over and you all go up in the air — hoof — like that?"

From the expression on Odette's face he immediately realised he had said it too brusquely; after all she was but a child.

"But, little French Odette, we have come over here to fight the Boche that are destroying your country, not to have the honour of a lovely tea made by your sweet hands."

Odette said she did not understand him, and for the next twenty minutes, with the help of a pocket dictionary, Mick unravelled the intricacies of his own sentiments about duty.

On the way back to the camp he remarked:

"Don't you think we're darned lucky to have found a sanctuary like that. I'm going to shoot that Hun down the next time — teach them they can't come over here with impunity."

Little did Mick realise when he said it that the fulfilment of his promise — or threat — was to be the stepping-stone that was going to lead him towards his magnificent achievements.

Two days later, sitting waiting high up over the lines, he attacked a two-seater and saw it go crashing down into our trenches near Avion. It may or may not have been the same one; in either case its destruction provided 'a corpse on our side of the lines'!!

Mick flew back to the Squadron and waited impatiently while a tender was being prepared to go up the line to salve what remained of the machine. He was flushed with excitement. At last he was able to prove what was 'within him'.

I did not see him until the evening, when he returned with several trophies from the wreck. His manner had undergone a change; excitement and conquest had apparently affected him so much that it was with some misgivings I went to his hut, after we had had a merry dinner in celebration.

He was sitting on his bed and as I stood leaning against the door he told me the whole story. The German machine, a D.F.W., had crashed into the trenches that had been occupied by the Germans before the battle of Arras. The pilot was dead and the observer, a captain, was wounded. In addition there was a dead dog beside the observer.

With great emotion Mick described the mangled condition of the pilot's body — blood and bones.

Horrified and disgusted with him I remarked reproachfully: "I'd never like to see the smashed-up body of a man I'd killed."

He looked at me queerly for a few seconds, then his eyes softened.

"Neither would I, old boy, it sickened me, but I wanted to see where my shots had gone. Do you know, there were three neat little bullet holes right here," pointing to the side of his head.

He then explained to me that he had fired his gun so often without hitting the enemy machines that he had begun to think that he could not *see* a target correctly. "No matter how much nausea it caused, I *had* to find out — and this one down our side was my only chance. I've missed so many of them, and I wanted to know for sure," he ended almost plaintively.

This made a tremendous impression on him as did the condition of the trenches through which he had had to pass. In their hurried advance the Canadians had not had time to bury the dead, and when I went up with Mick a few days later and saw and smelt the terrible aftermath of the attack, the impression it made on me was almost as strong as it had been on Mick. In hospital I had seen the tortured and shattered relics of a living battle, in the derelict trenches I saw the decomposing remains of a dead one. Here and there legs and arms were sticking out of the clay, some of them with khaki sleeves or puttees, others were but naked bones. Half-buried in the mud of the trench was a skull from which the flesh had been gnawed by the army of grey shapes that slunk away from us into the dug-outs. Over it all hung the overpowering, sickening stench of death.

The German dug-outs interested me particularly and, despite the danger of mine traps, Mannock and I explored several which had evidently not been touched since the day the Canadians had pushed the Germans out of the line. In one of these there were four dead Germans who had been smashed by a Mills bomb. The *concrete* walls were pitted where the bomb fragments had hit them.

There was one feature about Mick's first victim on our side of the lines which particularly annoyed us. The observer had been a captain but the pilot merely a N.C.O.

Mick drew us a picture of the noble 'Hauptman' driving his cowed N.C.O. over the lines at the point of the revolver — to earn the kudos for the *gallant*, one, the officer.

"Pity I didn't kill him instead of the poor pilot," were Mick's final words.

As Mick brought down another German on the next day his star began to rise in the mess and when, the following week, he succeeded in sending still another crashing to the ground, his future seemed assured. The G.O.C., General Trenchard, paid a visit to the Squadron, and Mick received his personal congratulations.

In the middle of a cheery lunch while entertaining the G.O.C.'s A.D.C. I was the unconscious cause of a good deal of merriment, and of discomfort to Major Tilney. I was ignorant of the name of the Commander-in-Chief of the R.F.C. and as I had only heard him referred to as 'Boom' I committed the terrible solecism of making some remark about 'General Boom'.

"General What!" his A.D.C. asked.

"General Boom!" I said so loudly that everyone heard.

There were titters round the table, and Major Tilney, who could never restrain his blushes, looked anxiously and angrily at us. The General himself, appreciating what had happened, laughed heartily and, to Tilney's relief, continued his conversation without making any comment.

During the next few weeks the aerial activity on the front increased and the flights were constantly being involved in scraps. One day the squadron was able to celebrate a 'bag' of four enemy machines. The old scrappers like Steve Godfrey, Mick, Zulu Lloyd, Hall, Blaxland, Lemon, Bond, Keen and Redler continued their destructive work (known officially as 'destroying') while the more junior members, Crole, Pettigrew, Kennedy, Rook and Barlow each accounted for several enemy machines.

We very rarely mentioned a success in mess, and unless we saw a combat report or the victor were an intimate friend, we did not even know who had been able to claim victorious combats. I heard the details of Crole's first one from Blaxland. They had encountered four Albatros near Douai, and in a desperate attack Crole had fired into one of them at point-blank range, to see it break in the air and plunge towards the ground in flames.

Spirits ran very high, for it appeared that after the terrible toll taken of our pilots during the Vimy push, we were wreaking vengeance on the enemy. As far as I could see it only meant that the Germans, becoming tired of seeing novices such as myself flying far over their side of the lines, had moved some of their fighters to our part of the line. At the same time they appeared to be rallying, for each morning they sent two-seater and fighter machines over our trenches. These did very little material damage, but the demoralising effect on our troops was considerable. The enemy machine would cross the lines at two or three hundred feet and every group of men or machine-gun emplacement would be used as a target. These raids took place at dawn when spirits are at their lowest ebb and, before long, headquarters realised that if the morale were to be maintained something must be done to stop them.

Bruay was eleven miles from the lines and as any preventive measure would involve machines taking off before it was daylight while the ground was practically invisible, we were provided with a landing-ground only a mile and a half from the trenches. The site chosen was a clover field about half a mile behind the village of Bully-Grenay and two miles south of Mazingarbe. For some reason or other we called the place 'Mazingarbe', while 43 Squadron, who occasionally used it, called it 'Petit Sains' after the farmstead of which the clover field formed part. Being within easy shelling distance it was not possible to build hangars, but a camouflaged tent, capable of covering two machines, was erected while a small wood-and-brick hut was built to house the wireless, the telephone, and to act as a 'doss house' for the pilots who were to carry out the patrols. We took turns at this unpleasant duty.

Being in full view of the enemy observation posts on 'Hill 70' we expected to be shelled every day, and only the two pilots on duty were allowed to land there. Ultimately, when it became apparent that the Germans were not going to pay us any particular attention, we made a habit of using the ground as a picnic place and taking-off pitch for lone flights.

Another clever idea that evolved itself from the possession of this 'stand-by' aerodrome right on the front was that of signalling the presence of enemy machines to pilots who were in the air. The enemy two-seaters were, as a rule camouflaged, and on a dull day it was exceedingly difficult for us to see such a machine when flying several thousand feet above it. To a ground observer the presence of the enemy was immediately obvious, and for this reason the landing-ground was provided with the wireless and telephone so that observers up in the trenches could report direct to the 'ground'. This raised a difficulty, for the ground observers could not be expected to give special signs nor could the pilots be expected to carry large maps, so that they might pin-point the position of the enemy. A remedy was required in the form of an 'Intelligent' officer on the landing-ground. This officer was to translate the pin-point reference into a single letter which could be laid out on the ground in strips of white canvas.

We had a good deal of amusement out of this, for a notice was posted in every squadron's mess in our Wing requesting volunteers for a special duty, and concluding '*the officer must be intelligent*'. No one in '40' had sufficient courage to claim to be intelligent and the officer who did undertake the duty resigned after a week. Constantly being referred to as the 'Intelligent Bloke' may have been too much for him. The scheme, both with this officer and with the mechanics who worked it later, was of great value to us. Within a minute of receiving a telephone call one of us could be in the air chasing after any venturesome two-seater which approached the lines.

At Mazingarbe we were nearer to the seat of the 'war'. Every afternoon Bully-Grenay was bombarded and occasionally shells landed on our clover field. This may have been because of a twelve-inch howitzer which was hidden behind a mound on the eastern side of the ground or because of three long-range naval guns on our right. The gigantic bellow of the howitzer deafened us every half-hour or so while, when they were active, the sharp yap, yap, yap of the naval guns reminded us that the enemy far on the other side of the lines was being kept on the qui vive. Both in front of us and to the north the ground appeared as if recurrent earthquakes had hit it; there was hardly a yard that did not carry some mark of the war: a shell-hole, a mine-crater, rusted barbed-wire entanglement, or the ruins of some house or hut. A railway had once run between Souchez and La Bassée, but this had long since been shelled to pieces; and near Mazingarbe were the rusted remains of an engine and train. The engine was lying on its side twenty yards from the line, a gaping rent in its boiler, while on the track opposite was a crater seven or eight feet deep.

All around us were signs of war's destruction. Bully-Grenay was but a litter of skeleton houses from which the roofs and floors had been blasted. During a bombardment we could see the clouds of red-brick dust rising from the ruins. Yet amidst all this desolation the philosophic owner of Petit Sains carried out his usual farmwork, sowing where he could and growing clover where ploughing was impossible.

Encouraged by success Mannock spent most of his time in the air and, in the evenings, shunning the mess, he frequently went off alone. Several times I saw him walking away, without having changed his flying boots, and a wave of sympathy would sweep over me. At other times, meeting the steely challenge of his piercing blue eyes and reading in them the mental turmoil that was going on within him, I became afraid of him. Mannock felt things much more keenly than the rest of us; his quick, emotional, Irish temperament made him live at a much higher pitch; there was so much more for him to see and feel. His soul was already raw where it had been lacerated by the sights he had seen. Instead of seeking his company I left him to fight out his terrific inward battle alone. He had shown that he could kill, not instinctively, but with deliberation, not for hatred, but for an ideal. It was civilisation turned topsy-turvy, and although the majority of us knew that the average Britisher needs but the unleashing of the bulldog that is in him to turn him into a killer, to Mick it came as a shock.

Zulu Lloyd, Keen, Godfrey and Mannock spent a good part of the day over on the German side of the lines chasing two-seaters and 'hawking' for unwary fighters. In the afternoons and evenings particularly, I carried out my own solo flights. The anti-aircraft shelling began to get on my nerves but, peculiarly enough, the sound of machine-guns failed to have any effect on me. My early escapades had given me confidence.

The tactics I employed were the same as those of the experienced fighters. I would cross the line at fifteen thousand or sixteen thousand feet, climb steadily to about nineteen thousand and then do a wide circle encompassing Douai, Henin Lietard and La Bassée. On the way, while calculating where the German gunners were likely to place each successive burst, I accustomed myself to watching everything that was going on in the line and on the German side. This practice in increasing my powers of observation stood me in good stead later on, but my principal object in consciously training myself was to avoid repeating the mistakes of the past. The quicker a pilot became accustomed to '*seeing*' everything that happened beside him, the greater was his efficiency and the better his chances of avoiding an untimely end.

Despite my cultivated alertness, on two occasions I missed what should have been easy victims. On the first of these I had a hard tussle with three Albatros and a two-seater, with no apparent result. Afterwards I 'sat' above a thin layer of cloud admiring the beauty of the sunset, and soothed my feelings by smoking a cigarette (strictly forbidden). The air was radiant with the red and gold of the sunset, the deep blue of the darkening sky, and my mind was filled with sweet thoughts of the original of a photograph I carried inside my cigarette-case. I had forgotten the war until I noticed that the red and gold of the sunset had almost disappeared. The sun was below the horizon and when its last rays were striking the clouds beneath me at seventeen thousand feet, I realised it must be almost dark on the ground.

On diving through the cloud, to my complete amazement I found myself only a hundred yards behind a German Albatros. Pulling up to get a good sight on him I held my fire until within about twenty yards. I was about to press the lever when he looked round abruptly and dived away, leaving my machine spinning in his 'wash'. My surprise at this was even greater than it had been on finding him. What made him look round at that particular moment when I was about to send him into eternity no one can ever know. Many pilots declared that there was a sixth sense that warned them of hostile thoughts near them.

On the other occasion, returning from a visit to Douai I saw a green-and-brown two-seater circling between Arras and the lines. lie was seven or eight thousand feet below me. Spiralling down in the twilight I had difficulty in keeping the machine in sight and when I flattened out I had to search for it, to find it only two hundred feet below me, flying east. The observer was staring straight up at me and, knowing that the pilot would make for the trenches as quickly as he could, I did a quick turn and dived.

Again the German disappeared in the thin mist and, despite my hurried dash towards the lines, I failed to see the machine again.

Cursing myself for being several types of fool I flew straight towards Lens with the intention of leaving the line when I reached the town. It was almost dark and, flying peacefully over the lines at eight thousand feet, I could see the flashes of the guns and of the bursting shells. All along both sides of the trenches there were the tell-tale flames of fire of the batteries and, as I had my map with me and could still make out the roads and woods, I began an interesting game of 'pin-pointing the enemy batteries'. The information would be useful to our own batteries.

I had located several small emplacements when, suddenly and without any movement on my part, my Nieuport turned a complete somersault and began to spin. On pulling her out of it the 'puppy dog' feeling again came over me. After having lost sight of a machine only two hundred feet from me I was prepared to believe that my mind was playing me tricks and that I must have stalled and caused the spin myself. I spotted a new flash exactly opposite me and my Nieuport did precisely the same thing. Only then the truth dawned on me. I was flying directly in the tracks of the shells, the draught from which was enough to blow my machine over.

More determined than ever to have my revenge by spotting more batteries, I descended to about four thousand feet and, as the flashes were becoming brighter with the increasing darkness, I managed to locate two more batteries. It was too dark to see my map sufficiently well to mark them, and I was folding it up when a dull 'woof' above me made me look upwards.

One or two hundred feet immediately overhead there was a beautiful fireworks display. Several thousand glowing balls were dropping straight towards me, leaving long columns of white smoke behind them. There was no alternative but to dive and to get out of the way, for the area covered must have been several hundred square yards. When completely clear of the streamers, I looked back to see a thin gossamer curtain of tapered white threads floating about in the air, the remains of an incendiary phosphorus shell.

The ground by this time was almost black and, with my nose well down, I flew with all speed to Bruay.

Having no lights to illuminate my instruments, and failing to see more than the dim outlines of the hangars, I made a very fast landing far out on the aerodrome. In the darkness I failed to see another machine standing in the middle of the landing-stretch and, catching sight of it only just in time, I had to put on full right rudder to avoid crashing into it. Purely by good luck my Nieuport fell back on her wheels after attempting to pirouette on her wing-tip, and as I climbed out hurriedly General Shephard and two mechanics ran up to me to see if I were hurt.

Our youthful Brigadier-General (he was thirty-one) explained that he had landed seven or eight minutes previously and had 'lost' his engine. While the mechanics were attempting to restart it they had heard the sound of my engine. "Run like Hell, Sir," one of the mechanics had said and, jumping out of his machine, the General had 'run like Hell' out of danger's way, accompanied by the mechanics.

Such incidents cemented the camaraderie that existed between all ranks of fighters in the R.F.C. Our Brigadier very frequently crossed the lines with us on special missions, and whenever an attack was in progress his Nieuport was to be seen hovering about, watching what was happening or taking his part in whatever engagements required his assistance.

About this time the changes in the Squadron seemed to be very rapid. Blaxland was sent to 'Home Establishment' for a rest as was Walder, while Captain Bath fell ill and had to go into hospital. He was replaced by Bond, but as the latter was on leave Redler led the 'A' flight patrols.

Redler was a particularly stout fellow and a capable leader and as we were such a small family we clung together all the closer. Bond's promotion was popular, and on his return there was a great celebration in the Squadron. My own interest in this, however, terminated when Barlow, in a friendly argument, laid me out with a water-jug.

On the morning of the 19th Zulu Lloyd and Crole were going into Bethune in a tender and, as they knew that I never missed an opportunity of a trip into one of the towns, halted the car outside 'A' flight hangar to let the driver hunt for me. I was preparing to go up on a flight when the driver told me and, thinking that an extra patrol over the lines might be more useful than a few drinks in Bethune, I was about to refuse when Corporal Godfrey, from the orderly room, came to ask where 'Mr. Mannock' was.

I knew Mick had just gone up and asked who wanted him.

Godfrey held out a telegram which said that 2nd Lieutenant Mannock had been awarded the Military Cross.

This made me change my mind about Bethune. Knowing that Mick was the last fellow to have anticipated the award of a decoration and that he was not likely to have any of the white and blue ribbon, I decided to get some from the depot in Bethune for him.

We completed our purchases quickly and returned in good time to allow me to have the ribbon sewn on Mick's tunic, which I hung prominently on the door of his hut before he landed.

No one was more astounded than he was when he heard the news. Second Lieutenant E. Mannock, M.C., sounded 'something like' as he himself might have said.

What that official recognition of his valour and 'devotion to duty' meant to Mick, only his best friends knew. His serious patriotism had been sullied by his consciousness of what he had called 'snobbery'. The award half persuaded him that, after all, things might not be so bad. This acted as an encouragement to him, not to gain more decorations, but to continue wholeheartedly to do his duty. In one way it helped him to get over the unpleasant transition that was taking place in his mind; it softened his bitterness and intensified his activities, giving him both actual and moral confidence in everything he did.

CHAPTER V

ON the evening of the 21st July, 'A' flight were over the lines on late duty. Towards the end of the two and a half hours' patrol the sun dropped below the horizon and, although the upper air was clear, the ground was covered by a slight haze which extended right to the horizon where it merged with the darkening eastern sky. To the north we saw a streak of flame against this filmy background, a dull flame which grew brighter as it dropped to the ground with a headlong rush, belching flames far behind it and leaving a column of almost invisible black smoke suspended in the air.

A flaming machine was a nauseating sight for any pilot. Such an ending was possible, if not probable, for every one of us because of the presence of flaming 'tracer' in the ammunition used by both sides, and the number of our pilots who, enduring agonies, had managed to land their machines after being hit had proved to us that having an incendiary bullet inside one's body was preferable to having it amongst the petrol. From the latter there was no escape, but unless a wound was fatal, an almost superhuman effort might save the life of the pilot in the former.

On seeing this flaming machine Bond flew as quickly as possible in the direction of the trail of smoke. On the way, fearing that Kennedy, flying behind me, might not be keeping watch I scanned the sky to our rear. Far away to the south there was another machine going down in the same way — a thin trail of flame and smoke. A machine diving to destruction was evidence that a combat had taken place. Bond, hoping to meet the enemy, circled round, but as our petrol was nearly finished he had to relinquish the search.

On landing we were horrified to hear that the first machine was one of No. 43 Squadron's Sopwith two-seaters and that the second one was Rook's.

Poor young Rook, we all prayed inwardly that he had been killed first. His gentle manner and imperishable smile had made him a general favourite. He was such a man's man, and we missed him at that night's game of poker.

There was a superstition in the Squadron that any pilot who played the scratched and battered piano that stood in one of the corners of the large mess would not live more than a week after he had touched the keys. Rook had played on the evening of Bond's 'dinner'. It was only on hearing of this on the night of Rook's death that I remembered the relief that had come over Mick's face when, in reply to his question, I expressed my regret for not being able to play. "Don't apologise, it's damned lucky you don't," he had said.

Hall, Steve Godfrey and Redler told me of several pilots who had been killed as justification for the superstition. None of us believed in it, but coincidence had played queer tricks with the Squadron, and continued to play them.

The next morning 'A' flight had to take the second patrol; and while we were arguing as to what positions we were to take, Redler and I maintaining that as we were likely to meet enemy flights it was better for us to take the rear positions in a 'V' formation, and Bond insisting that in an attack he wanted us alongside him, Major Tilney came over to warn Bond against taking too many risks. "Remember, it's a line patrol," we heard him say.

Bond was not the type that bothered much whether the patrol was officially 'Line' or 'Offensive'. There was only one type for 'A' flight, and as soon as we were over the trenches it was apparent that not only was our patrol going to be offensive, but that 'aggressively belligerent' would have described it more aptly. Bond had something to avenge. He led us straight over to Douai where we knew there were several German aerodromes; then, after circling round for a few minutes, dodging Archie, he tore off towards Cambrai, the next large town to the south-east. The same haze hung over the ground as on the previous evening, but the increasing warmth of the sun was dispelling it. The upper air was crystal clear, but the hazy horizon seemed to form the brim of a crucible in which our machines hung suspended. There were only the black puffs of the Archie bursts behind us to mar the sublime skyscape.

Half-way towards Cambrai, Bond turned round, heading north. To the west of Douai a captive balloon appeared above the haze, and as there was nothing else to attack, Bond gave a slow waggle of his wings and dived steeply towards the greenish-grey mass. A captive balloon looked more or less like a dirty, inflated, bulbous sausage, and as we dived I could see Bond changing the drum on his gun. At that time we carried three drums, one on the gun and two in the cockpit. One of these latter was filled with Buckingham, the incendiary bullets we used only on balloons.

The 'sausage' was five or six miles behind the lines and, in order that the observer in it might see far enough; the Germans had let it up to between six and seven thousand feet. We descended close to it, but at the last second for some reason or other Bond gave up the attempt after firing only a few rounds.

He then commenced to climb towards the lines, flying straight.

Redler was flying on his right with Kennedy behind him; I was on the left with Tudhope and Harrison behind me. Our speed, at the rate Bond was climbing, dropped to 80 m.p.h. and, with unpleasant recollections of the 'heavy gunner' into whose area we were approaching, I began to wonder why Bond was making no effort to mislead the enemy.

We had reached eight thousand feet when the first shells came up, right amongst us.

My machine was blown completely over, and on regaining control I saw that Bond had disappeared. Pieces of aeroplane fabric were whirling crazily in the air amidst the huge black smoke balls of the Archie bursts.

Incredulous I looked round for Bond, but he had gone; all that remained in the air were the stupid, dancing remnants of his planes.

Although I had been anxiously awaiting that first salvo from the deadly Archie gunner, his accuracy struck terror into me. One of the four shells, clustered only forty or fifty feet apart, had found its target in our Flight Commander's machine.

We pulled ourselves together and fell in behind Redler, but his machine too was obviously damaged. Half a minute later the cowling fell off the engine, and Redler, turning westwards, dived towards the lines. Fearing he might not reach our side, and with the knowledge that in the wilderness of shell-holes and barbed wire north of the Scarpe he would have little chance of landing safely, I followed him down to two thousand feet to see him crash into the shell-pitted ground on our side of the front line.

The patrol-time was not yet over, and as Tudhope, Harrison and Kennedy had continued alone, I flew north to Lens to meet them.

On landing we were relieved to hear that Redler was safe. Bond's certain death filled us with consternation. It was an unwritten code that we did not discuss the deaths of our friends, but the fact that the indomitable Bond had been killed by a direct hit from Archie meant more to us even than the loss of a friend. Everyone dreaded the savage bursting of the shells sent up to meet us by two gunners on the enemy front; our experience that morning taught us that our fears were not altogether unjustified. After having 'flirted' with Archie over the whole of our front on my solo patrols I had declared that one day either the gunner inside the Metallurgique works near La Bassée or the other between the Scarpe and Quiery would obtain a direct hit with his first burst. Poor Bond, had his enthusiasm possibly made him forgetful of this ever-present danger?

Later in the morning, really ignorant of what I intended to do, I asked my mechanics, Davidge and Biggs, to fill my tank, and while waiting for them to bring the petrol waggon my thoughts about the war and the Germans fell to the lowest dregs of bitterness. I had seen the wounded in hospital, the dead near Avion, had seen new pilot after new pilot arriving at the Squadron, had seen a bright promising youngster going down to a horrible death of flames, and had been within forty feet of my Flight Commander when his machine was shattered in a savage, black, shell-burst.

I remembered my own squeamishness on seeing the Albatros going down in flames. Anyway, I had got *him* properly.

It was then a fiendish idea came into my mind. The German pilots, as far as I saw, used only incendiary ammunition. When they hit us we were 'finished', but two or three mornings previously I had emptied a drum of our own clean ammunition into a two-seater without any apparent effect. I decided to remedy this by a concoction of my own, by filling my drums with the three types of ammunition, 'armour piercer', 'tracer' and Buckingham (incendiary). Such a mixture would certainly prevent the next enemy's escaping.

The first indication of the level to which my 'morality' had fallen was provided by Davidge. He was a very clever mechanic, much older than myself; his greyish hair always gave me the idea that our positions should have been reversed as far as rank was concerned. He did not refuse to fill my drums as I wanted, he drove it home to me much more effectively.

"I'll do it if you order me to, Sir, but if you are caught with such ammunition on you it will mean death for you on the other side and court martial for me here."

Determined to have my 'mixture' and prepared to accept full responsibility I carried my three drums over to the armoury hut and locked myself inside.

It took me ten minutes to fill the first drum, for I had to lay the cartridges out in order, and test each for a sunken or defective 'cap'. This was a frequent cause of stoppages, and as it very often jammed the gun beyond remedy in the air, we had to take every precaution. Cursing the Germans, the Kaiser, and the profiteering manufacturers who made it necessary for us to examine the ammunition that had been 'passed' in the munitions factories, I was surprised to hear a timid knock at the door.

I asked who it might be, and Mannock's voice replied: "Let me in, I want to speak to you."

On my opening the door for him, he came inside, shut the door slowly after him and stood leaning against the post.

Conscious that I was doing something 'dirty' I could feel the tension in the air as I waited for him to speak first.

"What are you doing there?" he asked, knowing very well, because he added, "Your mechanics have just told me."

"Mixing some filth and corruption for the Huns," I said angrily, "I'm going to make sure of the next one I hit."

Filling the remainder of the drum, mechanically, 'one tracer, one armour piercer, one Buckingham', I glanced at him several times without meeting his eyes. Something had upset him, his face was haggard and he was nervously pulling the strap of his Sam Browne.

When I was about to commence filling the third drum he put his hand on my arm. He was trembling.

"Look here, Mac. If you have any affection for me, forget about last night and this morning and let me empty out that stuff."

I stopped and sat down on the bench, facing him.

"It isn't only poor old Rook. They've never fired anything at me but incendiary; and two mornings ago I missed a two-seater. If I had had my drums loaded with this I'd have got him — properly."

He stood silently looking at me — almost tearfully and, in support of my own wavering brutality, I continued:

"I'm out to do as much damage as I can and the surest way, no matter what it means, is the best for me. Besides — it isn't like you to care about how they die as long as we kill them."

Again his challenging eyes met mine: "Do you mean to say, Mac, that you would coolly fire that muck into a fellow-creature or, worse still, into his petrol tank, knowing what it must mean?"

I realised then that the hardening effect of the war had been greater on me than on Mick; or that he was attempting to play on my emotions.

"Well, if I can't do anything with you I may as well go and leave you to it, but I'll give you one last chance. If you won't chuck it for humanity, will you for me?"

He had come down to our old footing. "If *you* will tell me exactly why you are so upset about it," I replied.

His eyes filled with tears. "Because that's the way they're going to get me in the end — flames and finish. I'm never going to have it said that my own right hand ever used the same dirty weapons."

Poor old Mick. He was so obviously in a highly strung emotional state that I laughed. "All right, you darned old sentimentalist, if that's how you feel about it, I'll empty my drums."

He took my arm saying, "No, let the 'mechs' do it," and as we walked up and down outside I chaffed him about his fear, telling him that on seeing Rook's machine and the Sopwith going down in flames we had all been filled with the same dread.

"No, Mac," he replied. "They'll never be able to 'get' *you*, but as sure as I'm talking to you now, that's the way they're going to finish me. The other fellows all laugh at my carrying a revolver, think I'm doing a bit of play-acting in going to shoot a machine down with it, but they're wrong — the reason I bought it was to finish myself as soon as I see the first sign of flames."

To shun sentiment and emotion is the keynote of our British upbringing, yet this outburst from Mick did not embarrass me. I never expected him to bend in obeisance to humbug. He was not fettered by our false social ethics, his natural humanity and the spontaneity of both his mental and physical reactions was as refreshing to me as a draught of cool clear spring water in a room fouled by the fumes of smoke and wine. He was, at that time, groping about for some guiding principle in life, in civilisation, and in his eagerness he clutched at anything that resembled an ideal in concrete form.

After lunch Redler asked me into the hut he had shared with Bond. He told me that he and Bond had had an agreement that if anything serious happened to one, the other would write to his next of kin. Bond was married, and Redler, in fulfilment of his promise, had to write to Mrs. Bond.

"I've got to pack his things too," he said.

Both of us knew that there was no hope of Bond's having survived, but to say so bluntly without having seen his dead body miles on the other side of the line was more than Redler could bring himself to do.

Whilst he was writing and reading over the sentences for my criticism, I sat on Bond's bed sorting out his belongings, his books, his clothing, his manuscript; and when I came to his shaving-kit and a few delicate souvenirs of his happiness with his wife, the terrible loneliness of all of us was amply impressed on my mind. When we went, we were reported as 'Missing and sometimes 'Missing reported killed if our fellow-pilots had the nerve to say that we had definitely been seen going down in such a condition that death was certain. Afterwards, some friend would pack the belongings that were no more use to us, the shaving-brush with the morning's soap still wet on it, the diary, the letters from friends and the photographs; all to make room for another pilot who might share the same fate within a week or a month.

Even Major Tilney, who usually tried to keep up the spirits at dinner, succumbed to the general depression, and afterwards he and Keen departed to see some friends.

When Squadron orders were posted we learnt that Mick was to command 'A' flight. The news was not welcomed by some of the others in the Squadron, and as Mick had disappeared there was a good deal of criticism of his promotion. Despite his undoubted ability he had not 'lived down' his reputation of being slightly 'yellow'.

'What had got him his decoration had been the spectacular effect of the two-seater on our side of the line. Other fellows had done much more without any recognition.'

'He was "soft", and pandered to the C.O. and the staff while several with much more courage and ability avoided the non-combatant groundsmen who could give decorations and promotion.'

'Mick was a mad lone fighter who would only lose his head with success.'

'He was not fit to command a flight.'

These criticisms and much more I had to hear and, despite my protestations, remembering what Mick had told me, I had to admit that there was some truth in what had been said.

Knowing the phases through which Mick had passed, I wondered if promotion would prove too much for his mental equilibrium. I doubted whether he would take it quietly.

On the next morning, sure enough, his high spirits were immediately evident. We followed behind him in a frantic drive for Valenciennes, nearly thirty miles on the other side of the line. There we circled round and returned towards the lines via Douai and Henin Lietard. Mick was on the qui vive looking out for low-flying enemies, but there was nothing on which he could lead his flight. Excitement at the promotion, combined with the knowledge that four or five other pilots were bound to follow wherever they were led, may have induced a feeling of power and a greater determination to meet the enemy. Mick's behaviour, however, annoyed me; it bore out several of the things that had been said about him. I had hoped that he would take things quietly until the flight became accustomed to him.

Filled with disgust at seeing in my friend what I thought was another manifestation of the wrong side of the war mentality, I determined to leave the patrol as soon as opportunity offered. We had been flying at twelve to thirteen thousand feet, about three thousand feet below a heavy bank of cumulus clouds. Returning from a second trip to the north of La Bassée, Mick climbed until Redler and I were forced to fly intermittently through the lower parts of the clouds. Flying like this we should have been particularly easy prey for any enemy fighters that might be cunning enough to stalk us from above the clouds, and with this fear as a plausible excuse I flew straight up through the cloud the next time my machine was enveloped in it.

Above the clouds the sun was shining down on an endless quilt of snow-white billows and, climbing clear of the upper hummocks of the cloud, two or three hundred feet above the main bank, I saw two machines several miles to the east. They were large two-seaters, and as they approached were easily recognisable as German. 1 flew to meet them, hoping to see the flight coming up through the clouds, and climbing so that I might have a chance to attack the two-seaters from above.

They also climbed and, determined to attack them, I zoomed two or three times until almost on their level. Still there was no sign of the flight to assist me and, fearing I was going to fail to reach the two-seaters, I opened fire at long range, gradually pulling my Nieuport up until it was almost underneath the leading enemy. As the last round from the drum left the barrel my machine stalled, making me almost a stationary target for the enemy. My shots must have had some effect on the first one; he turned away and dived east, but as my machine fell gently with the controls perfectly loose, the observer in the second machine, which had then passed me, fired his slow pop-pop-pop in my direction, his bullets exploding over a hundred feet from me.

My machine had dived, spinning into the cloud before I regained control, and on straightening out the clouds were above me. A cloud of Archie bursts several miles west of me showed where Mannock was. While changing drums preparatory to climbing back through the clouds to find the second two-seater, I saw the first one going down in a long steep dive towards Courcelles.

Flying through a dense cumulus cloud everything quickly becomes damp and the noise of the engine is deadened. This one was so thick that I could not see my wing-tip, and in such circumstances had no idea what my machine was doing. Flying blind and wondering whether I were going to come out above or below the cloud, I heard the dull, ghostly 'woof' of the anti-aircraft shells exploding all round me. The German gunners provided me with one of the eeriest experiences of my life, and as the thick heavy wet cloud seemed interminable three more salvos had exploded before I emerged on top of it.

The enemy two-seater had disappeared and, being many miles on the German side and having been up for nearly two hours and a half, I flew back to Bruay as quickly as possible.

Being accustomed to flying alone I had almost forgotten that we had been on an official patrol until I was filling in my report. Mick was standing at the door, watching me, but when I had finished, instead of speaking, he walked away dangling his flying cap against his right leg. Again that feeling of sympathy and pathos came over me, and I regretted having 'let him down' before the others by openly rebelling against his leadership and taking the initiative into my own hands.

In the afternoon Redler and I were still parcelling Bond's effects and labelling them, while Mick, sitting on the door-step of his hut, was scribbling as fast as he could. In *King of Air Fighters*, a letter he wrote that day is quoted, illustrating his excitement, "Secret! Got the M.C., old boy, and made Captain and Flight Commander on probation. Don't tell anyone and still write me as the usual Lieutenant."

We did another patrol before dinner, and I did not have a chance to speak to him alone until the evening. He was wearing his light-coloured shirt and was carrying a cane (an unusual thing for him). He passed once or twice between the gate and the tennis court. I was writing in my hut and, seeing him obviously trying to attract my attention, called out:

"Want your constitutional, Mick?"

He came over to the door slowly. "Yes, all right, if you want to come — with your Flight Commander." We both laughed. I knew he had forgiven me, but could not help saying, "Yes, I don't think a serious talk will do either of us any harm."

"All right then, old boy — hurry up."

He did not speak until we were half-way towards the town, then very quietly, "You hurt me like hell this morning, Mac! Why did you leave the flight?" I thought of lying to him, but his directness, his disarming way of laying himself at his friend's mercy, made me reply, just as quietly, "Because I *meant* to hurt you."

I told him how much I admired his courage and his brain and how glad I was to see him getting his reward, but that, seeing the change that had come over him, I was afraid that the ingenuous fellow who took me in hand when I joined the Squadron had shown that he had, after all, only the ordinary standard of values. The fact that he had achieved a little advance made no difference to me: I had always valued the man, in favour or disrepute, for what was in his mind.

He began to argue with me, but then I reminded him of what he had said the first night about what a man 'had in his head and his guts' and asked him if his own ideals were as steadfast as he had considered them to be. Pointing to the white-and-blue ribbon underneath his wings, I said, "Don't tell me that that makes any difference to what you think of yourself."

He thought for a few moments, then said, "Hell, none at all. Come on, old son, you win every time. I suppose it's because you've been to university. I'm going to study."

We had followed the same road as on our first walk and, arriving back in Bruay, I asked him into Odette's, as we called the estaminet, to drink his success. Odette was there, and Mick, with his usual enthusiasm for learning French from such a charming teacher, forgot all about me after Odette and I had 'toasted' his 'Command'.

The sentiments concerning his promotion had not died down when we got back to the Squadron and, as everyone was sitting on the tennis court listening to the gramophone, several shafts were fired at him.

One, a particularly nasty dig, from a fellow for whom I had the greatest respect, Mick could not let go unchallenged, "It's about time a real man went down to see about that fair-haired bit of stuff in the estaminet."

Mick flared up. Everyone knew who the fair-haired one was.

"Anyone that tries to muck about with that child will have his head knocked off."

There was a loud guffaw in reply.

"And who'll do the knocking?" the pilot asked.

To save Mick the trouble, I said immediately, "I will."

The tables were turned and everyone laughed. After the affair of the first patrol they had hardly expected me to support Mick.

This drove home to me my real perfidy in having left him that morning. His principal antagonist was also a friend of mine, and when he tackled me later about my change of front and tried to point out that Mick had frequently shown signs of timorousness and that as far as promotion was concerned I myself was more worthy, I told him of my high opinion of Mick. This pilot was recognised as a prince of good fellows but, like most of us, he never stopped to enquire whether or not another pilot were showing signs of being merely cautious or cowardly; he had mistaken the cause of Mick's delay in joining the first dog-fights. Unless we knew a pilot very well all that worried us were the outward manifestations. I knew that both Mick and his principal antagonist were fine fellows in their own ways, Mick's nature being the more sensitive of the two, and it was a great pleasure to me when I was able to bring them together to 'have it out'.

In any case, before a week had elapsed, Mannock had proved both his ability and his courage beyond all doubt.

Redler had spent over six months with the Squadron, and as the doctor found out that he had been suffering from a complaint that several tried to conceal — bleeding from the nose — he was sent home for a rest and to act as fighting instructor to a training squadron.

After Bond's death Hall had shared Redler's hut, and as both Hall and I had huts to ourselves Hall invited me to take Redler's place, in case a new pilot were 'inflicted' on one of us. On the day after Redler's departure we spent all our spare time moving my decorations and fittings, and by tea-time the hut was completed. Having been in the corner, the other fellows had not noticed the interior of my hut, but as Hall's faced directly on to the tennis court, its luxurious fittings could no longer escape notice.

The unsightly brown canvas was covered with blue cretonne, the wash-stand was made more decorative by means of checked oil-cloth and a curtain, a bookcase was erected on top of a writing table, and the Kirchner and other pictures were arranged suitably round the walls with 'Kaloma' at the end. In addition, we provided chintz curtains for the windows, and mats for the floor. The whole transformation had cost seven or eight pounds and, whilst Hall and I were working on it, tacking the cretonne to the struts and pretending to be taking a rather 'effeminate' interest in our artistic household effects, the others paid us frequent visits to jeer at our optimism and our comfort.

When we saw the hut after dinner, someone had hung a large placard over the door, 'THE BROTHEL'.

Redler's departure caused a vacancy in the flight, and Major Tilney's confidence in Mannock was amply demonstrated by the fact that Tudhope was definitely transferred to 'A' flight, and the new pilot took Tud's place.

Tudhope was a particularly brave scrapper, and before long Mick, Tud and I were almost inseparable. With Kennedy and Harrison, we carried out our duty patrols of keeping the line clear of enemy flights, with occasional raids on the area between Douai and La Bassée. Occasionally all three of us would go up together, but usually we preferred to be alone. There was much more chance of the Germans waiting to fight a lone flier, and during the remainder of July all the enthusiasts of the Squadron, Zulu, Steve, Crole, Keeno and 'George' joined in a 'push' to keep the sky clear of German aircraft.

The enemy must have thought we were mad, for frequently one of us would circle over their aerodromes and 'stunt On one such occasion, performing all the gyrations of which a Nieuport was capable at fifteen thousand feet over the Douai aerodromes for the amusement and demoralisation of the German fliers and anti-aircraft gunners, I saw a silver Albatros spinning from about my level near Valenciennes.

Thinking it was a German also amusing the ground forces, I flew towards him, watching and wondering when he was going to straighten out. The rhythmic turns and stalls of the spin soon made me realise that the pilot was not controlling the machine and, after what seemed an endless suspense, 1 saw it hit the ground, to perish in a cloud of smoke and flames. When it had commenced spinning, it had been two or three miles distant, and as it was my invariable rule never to report on solo flights unless confident I had had a 'confirmable' conquest, I did not say anything about this Albatros until Keen came into the mess twenty minutes after me.

"Have you just been up, Keeno?" I asked.

"Yes," he replied, sitting down wearily in a rickety wicker arm-chair.

On asking him if he had seen the silver Albatros spinning into the ground he jumped straight out of his chair.

"Did you see it — where were you?"

I told him what I had been doing and what I had seen.

"Did you report it?" he asked.

"No, it was 'away to hell an' gone' near Valenciennes. Why?"

"Because I 'did it in'. I've just handed in my report, but there won't be any confirmation because it was so far on the other side." He looked at me reproachfully. "You are a damned old fool, Mac. Through this beastly reticence of yours you've lost me a lonely Hun."

Mick heard this and offered to put the case before the C.O., but Keen would not allow it. "We've got our rules about reports being given in without collusion and we can't go against it. I wouldn't ask even although you fellows know."

We all recognised Keen as the best type of Englishman, courageous, modest, clever, yet with that aloofness which many people mistook for superciliousness. His next remark showed how little the loss of the glory of a 'confirmed one' had affected him.

"By gum — you must have wonderful eyesight, Mac. I didn't see any other machine in the sky."

Keen, Mannock and I used Mazingarbe as a rendezvous, and occasionally we found Zulu Lloyd, Steve, Hall, Pettigrew, or Tudhope there. We arranged amongst ourselves that one of us should 'mount guard' on the ground while the others were scouting around. The clover was becoming rather long, and the sweet smell of the flowers brought back memories of my childhood. We frequently had tea or even dinner there, the latter consisting of tinned lobster. A whole case of this delicacy, of which we had grown tired in the mess, had been dumped at Mazingarbe, and anyone who felt hungry could always have a tin if he were prepared to take the risk of ptomaine poisoning.

The work we performed from Mazingarbe was entirely voluntary; in effect, we were the self-appointed special-constables of the front. The German two-seaters were cautious, and when they crept up near the line, one of our O.P.s would telephone to us and immediately a machine would depart to harass the German and prevent him from co-operating effectively with his artillery. We occasionally succeeded in catching the Germans, and the general effect of this work was that the Germans were unable to register proper targets on our side of the line. Owing to his inability to locate correctly the battery or dump, whichever it may have been, Jerry was forced to bracket his targets by placing bursts on all sides and then in the middle — an expensive business. Very frequently, if too many of us were there, one or two would go off on more belligerent flights, crossing the lines in the south and approaching them again from the east in such a way that we might catch a two-seater that was not paying sufficient attention to his 'tail'. From the spectacular and destructive aspect these flights were more successful.

One afternoon, while telephoning the report of a scrap I had had, I heard loud shouts outside and heard Mannock's machine taking off in great haste. A minute later, on leaving the hut I saw him about a mile away to the south-east, chasing an Albatros.

The two machines were at five hundred feet, with Mannock's Nieuport just behind the German. At that height their speed appeared to be tremendous, but the German was the faster of the two and as he had the lead there should have been every possibility of his escaping. Mannock was determined and, knowing the German's advantage, used every 'ounce' both of his machine and his ability. Every time the German flew straight for two seconds Mick's gun spat, forcing the Albatros to twist and turn to avoid the bullets. It was like a hare being chased by a greyhound, and as it took place at a terrific speed we stood breathless and fascinated by the sight. The German, realising Mick had him beaten, rounded on his pursuer and for a moment it appeared as if there were going to be a fight, but Mannock, pulling his machine up in a zoom, sent a final burst into the Albatros.

The plucky German crashed straight into the trenches, and two minutes later Mick landed on Mazingarbe.

"Got him, by Jove. Our side, too," and asking me to report it to Bruay, he took the tender and dashed off towards Bully-Grenay.

Again his spirit, determination, quickness and marksmanship had been rewarded.

The German was not dead, but three of Mick's bullets had lodged in his arm and leg. This stout fellow, by name Von Bartrap, had come over to attack one of our balloons but, failing in the first attempt and seeing Mannock climbing to cut him off, had considered that retreat was the safest policy. He was wearing the Iron Cross, but despite this evidence of past victorious combats, unfortunately for him, he had not been quick enough for the determined Mannock.

In celebration of this event Mick, Tudhope and I decided to have a special dinner in Amiens, and as someone had to fetch a new machine from Candas we seized the opportunity of getting a tender without having to admit that we were holding our celebration away from the Squadron. We had been fighting every day, but another 'body' alive or dead on our side of the lines was an event. Even although shooting down an enemy machine under such conditions was considered 'killing cold meat' we had our own special reasons for wanting to be together. With Mick as Flight Commander we felt very much as if we belonged to one family, our two younger brothers Kennedy and Harrison still being considered as learners.

We obtained a table at the 'Belfort' and Mick, after choosing the dinner, ordered champagne. When the waiter had disappeared he leant over the round table towards me:

"Tell you what we'll do," he whispered confidentially. "Old Richthofen is supposed to be on Dorignies aerodrome; let's raid the blooming place to-morrow."

Both Tud and I agreed but, thinking that Mick was painting the projected stunt too vividly, I told him that although I had sat over Douai and Waziers several times I had seen only two red Albatros (the type of machine Richthofen's Circus was supposed to fly). I told them that in my opinion the

'Richthofen scare' was a myth and the cleverest piece of propaganda the Germans had 'put over on us'.

Mick pretended to be furious.

"I knew you'd kick the guts out of the thing, reduce it to an ordinary bit of flying; but you don't see the moral of it. We three are going over their aerodrome, they're our particular opponents, and if we fly round at a thousand feet we can take turns at 'doing them in' as they try to take off. We'll 'learn 'em' even their home aerodromes aren't safe."

We were carried away by enthusiasm for the strafe and, drinking damnation to Richthofen and his red Albatros, we finished a merry meal, which further cemented the strong bond of understanding and comradeship that was to bind us together for the rest of the year.

To be back at Bruay in time for the raid necessitated leaving the ground at Candas at the break of dawn, and on 'pulling matches' to decide which of us was to do it, I lost. Before parting with Mick and Tud, I extorted a promise from them that they would not 'take off' without me.

"All right, old boy, we'll hold up the murder till you come back," Mick called out.

Unfortunately for me, we had reckoned without the lie-a-bed tendencies of the Candas staff.

It was six o'clock before I awoke, and I hurried on to the aerodrome without having had breakfast. A thick white morning mist on the ground necessitated my taking off on the longest run of the aerodrome.

The mechanics had carelessly fitted the machine with a heavy Sopwith two-seater cowling instead of the light Nieuport one, and, with this extra weight to hold her down, the new machine would hardly leave the ground. The run seemed interminable, and I had barely room to hop over the almost invisible hedge at the far side. On the other side of the hedge my wheels hit the ground again before the nose-heavy Nieuport would take the air properly. Even then I flew to Bruay with the joy-stick fully pulled back, reaching our aerodrome, the only ground visible above the carpet of mist, at two thousand feet.

Mannock and Tudhope had gone up taking Kennedy in my place, and as I was expostulating fairly luridly about their perfidy to Sergeant Smart, the sergeant fitter, we heard the sound of their engines.

Mick, with his three streamers flying defiantly, landed first and taxied in furiously without waiting for the mechanics to run out to him. When the machine stopped, instead of getting out boisterously as he was accustomed to do, he sat still in the cockpit with his head clasped between his hands.

At my approach he lifted his head and held up his hand to silence my inevitable outburst.

"It's all right, old Mac, I'm damned sorry. I'll never do it again. I've had all the gruelling I want this morning, my God, never had such a wind-up in my life."

Tud and Kennedy landed, and Mick, watching them taxi-ing in, said: "Thank God they've got back. Poor old Tud must be shot to hell."

Tud's machine was in such a condition that it might have been sent to a flying school to act as an inspiration and a warning to budding fighters. An explosive bullet had burnt through his main spar a few inches from the 'V' strut, one of his top planes had been cut to ribbons by bullets, every one of his instruments was smashed, and a bullet had passed through his coat collar. Tud's face was a study, it depicted a combination of cynicism and amusement. He had certainly been very close to death that morning.

Kennedy had fared better, but his fuselage and planes carried many mementoes of the fury of the fight in which they had been engaged.

"Get any of *them*?" I asked Mick.

They could not see any humour in this question at the time, although they laughed over it later.

"No," Mick replied ruefully, "my only concern was to save my blooming skin. I thought they *had* all of us. Thank God we're back anyway."

It transpired that on crossing the lines towards Douai they had encountered nine enemy scouts flying in formation. Mick, intent on 'showing 'em' had waded right into the Germans, only to be met with a vigorous resistance, from which he had been only too glad to escape. The Germans also, finding they could not destroy the three Nieuports, considered that the 'victory was not assured'. On rallying with Tud and Kennedy, Mick had the joy of seeing them scattering and flying off east — their noses well down and 'their tails properly between their legs' as he described their attitude.

This fright taught Mannock — and the rest of us — several important matters that affected our future conduct. The Germans were not by any means the incompetent and cowardly pilots we had imagined. No matter how courageous we might be, it was of little avail going helter-skelter into a fight with every advantage on the other side. Although Mick himself, by adopting purely defensive tactics when surrounded by the Germans, had escaped, it was only luck that had allowed Tud and Kennedy to get back. Tudhope, thinking that Mick was attacking, had concentrated too much on 'getting' one of their opponents without considering the consequences to himself.

On the way round to the camp Mick was so despondent that I felt it necessary to do something to cheer him up. A reverse that was allowed to get on his nerves might have done him irremediable harm.

"Well, anyway, you have one consolation. Think of the moral effect on the troops of seeing three of you wading into nine of them; and chasing them too. Besides, there's the demoralising effect on the Huns themselves. Teach them they can't damned well fly in *our* sky when we're around."

Mick stopped and called to Harrison who was walking with Kennedy behind us.

"Here, you two, ''ark at' what Mac's got to say!"

His temperament responded so quickly to any stimulus, particularly an optimistic one, that when I had repeated the remark he linked arms with us.

"Come on, let's have a drink. We'll chase the Huns out of *our* sky. That's our motto now." Mick had passed another milestone along his career. Discussing the scrap with him that night he told me that for the first time he had realised that his friends' lives were in his hands and that as Flight Commander he could not behave as an individualist. "I don't want to lose any of you," he said, "but Tud's so damned keen on getting at *them* he forgets about his own tail. You'll have to look after him for a bit." I told him that in my opinion Tud's experience had been all that was necessary to make him careful, but Mick expostulated.

"No, neither you, nor I, nor the Huns will ever do it. It will have to come from Tud himself."

At the end of our walk as we passed the hangars he took my arm: "You old blighter, they'll never get you."

Remembering what he had told me about his own premonition, I asked him if he thought he were really psychic.

"I often get feelings, true feelings," he replied. "You're going to come through all right, but Ken and Harrie won't, that's definite. I'm not quite sure about Tud. I hope none of their deaths will ever be laid at my door."

This seemed to worry him for some time, and I noticed that he was more inclined to manoeuvre into a suitable position before attacking. Immediately he flew into an attack, however, his caution disappeared, he left it to me to look after the security of the others.

After the vicissitudes of the past fortnight the flight was beginning to develop into an efficient fighting unit.

I felt that my two months of training, of learning the character and psychology of war, had made me better equipped and more competent to take my part in the general conflict and in the progress of the flight.

CHAPTER VI

IT was probably because I was becoming inured to the dangers and horrors of war that at the end of July, and more particularly the beginning of August, the whole scheme gradually appeared more intelligible to me. Fighting was no longer a cause for excitement, it was our work. While flying at eighteen thousand feet over Armentières on a clear day we could see the battlefields extending right to the coast, while, to the south, we could see the dim haze that always hung over the Somme area.

At Ypres a long battle was being waged amongst the shell-hole puddles and watery canals of the trenches. We were frequently ordered to carry out special patrols over the battle-front, which gave us a chance of examining the water-logged country. For miles the ground looked like a swamp, a morass of miniature lakes and rain-sodden trenches in which the troops were waging an interminable and miserable war.

General Trenchard placed great faith in the moral effect of allowing us to carry on an aggressive war, it encouraged the other arms and securely established our aerial supremacy. There had been a great deal of scaremongering about Richthofen and his Circus, and the attitude of older pilots towards this supposed menace had a great deal to do with the maintenance of our spirits. We knew that the German 'Knight' was but a 'bogy man' and that the Germans, with very few exceptions, never took any risks. The only occasion on which I met red Albatros which I believed belonged to the 'Circus' was between Douai and Cambrai. These attacked me with vigour, but on finding that I was not exactly 'easy meat' retired to a discreet distance and escorted me back to the lines. For over ten miles they had every chance of attacking me, but the energy I had put into my effort to come to close quarters evidently persuaded them that this was another occasion on which 'victory was not assured'.

When, however, one did meet confident Germans there was no more terrifying experience, and only the superior stunting powers of our Nieuports and the control we had over them allowed us to get home safely. The attitude towards us of such Germans amply bore out what I had always propounded as the real reason for our fighting them; the hatred of their 'Hunnish Kultur', of their ruthlessness and of their machine-like precision which took no account of human emotions nor even of character values. They worked on a cold philosophy, a cruel one, that required officers to drive their men onwards at the point of the revolver. Only outstanding pilots such as Voss and Boelke possessed the spirit that could lift them above the 'machine' of which they were supposed to be part. We were ever conscious of being opposed by an inhuman weapon, the method, the system and the logic of an almost invincible foe; yet we could never get them to fight on the level. In the air we forced from them the admission of our superiority.

Mick, Keen, Zulu, and I frequently had arguments about this. I never admitted having any *hatred* of the Germans as individuals; there had been several at university with me, decent fellows, and, knowing something of the different standards of morality and 'sportsmanship' between them and the British, I did not call the enemy cowards. This frequently made Mick furious, particularly after seven or eight Albatros had refused to face a combat with the flight. He could never see that 'morale', the great French word we had adopted, meant nothing to the German.

Failing entirely to understand my outlook he ceased using the word *Him* and referred to them as 'your pals'. Becoming exasperated one evening at his sneering at 'Mac's b——y pals' in mess, I took him to my hut and 'had it out'.

I told him the Germans were playing what we were entitled to call a cowardly *game*, but that war ought to be no more a sport to us than it was to them. Their policy was clever, but if we were wise we could still beat them at it. Most of the casualties in our (and other fighter) squadrons were novices, and to prevent serious losses we must *train* our fellows to do as much damage as possible without taking undue risks.

This talk had a great effect on Mick. He spoke of the Germans as 'old Fritz' or 'Jerry', and instead of going off alone he originated a plan by which he would take Harrison with him while I took Kennedy. Tud was to act as supernumerary. At the same time he decided that we were to study attacking in formation instead of the dangerously straggling method we had been forced to adopt because of the haphazard way Mick himself dived into enemy formations. We practised this on patrols, and one morning, having carried out several mock onslaughts on an imaginary enemy, we were heading for Henin Lietard when we met another Nieuport, flown by Zulu Lloyd. For some minutes we carried on a sham fight with him until the Archie became too accurate. On sorting ourselves out we noticed that Mick had 'fallen in' behind Zulu, who headed due east towards Valenciennes.

The air was lucidly clear, and when we were some distance from the town I saw five dark shapes moving about near the ground. Zulu wagged his wings, and the four of us, Mick, Tud, Kennedy and I, closed in on him. From seventeen thousand feet we dived, south-east first so that we could get between the enemy and the sun, and then due north, towards them. Even before we had descended to their level of five or six thousand feet I realised that there was something wrong. The German machines were two-seaters, and before we got within range they had flown round a complete rectangle, flying in perfect formation.

Coming down close to the enemy, Zulu dived straight for the leader while we each singled out our counterpart in the other flight. I prepared myself to face the effects of the 'nasty sting', but strangely enough the observer allowed me to reach point-blank range without showing any signs of defending himself. I got the engine of the machine properly into position in my Aldis and immediately opened fire. The tracer shot straight into the cockpits, each flame accompanied by ten invisible armour piercers. The heavy greenish-grey two-seater dived away, obviously out of control. Only then the truth dawned on me. The observer had been clear in my sight, he had been looking at me, but he had made no attempt to fire, because *he had no gun*. The flight had evidently been practising formation flying and, being low down so far from the front, had never thought of the possibility of attack.

On returning to Bruay, Mick jumped out of his Nieuport and with a wild whoop threw his flying cap into the air.

"Here, steady on!" I yelled.

"What the Pygmalion!" he called back. "What's wrong with *you*?"

He came over to my machine as Kennedy taxied in.

"You cold-blooded murderer," I said quietly, almost accusingly.

"What the blazes do you mean! Five blinking Huns in one morning!"

"Yes, five blinking Huns without any guns," I replied in the same tone, laughing outright at his bewildered expression. "Those machines had no guns on them. We shot down a lot of pupils. That's the nearest approach to cold-blooded murder I've ever seen."

He was immediately serious, and as Tud and Kennedy joined us I asked them if any of the Germans had fired at them.

It was true, not one of the German observers had had a gun, so Mick called to Zulu who was leisurely climbing out of his machine.

"Mac says those two-seaters weren't armed, and I'm inclined to agree with him. What do you say?"

Zulu had been smiling, but after scratching his head, his round cheery face wrinkled into a frown.

"I think they were *pupils*," I remarked.

"That explains it then. I thought there was something tame about the whole thing," Zulu said, and after a few seconds, "But look here then, we can't damned well hand in combat reports."

Zulu was always prepared to do the chivalrous act in his own unassuming way.

"It was pure cold-blooded murder," I said, laughing at the shock to the others' sporting instincts.

Zulu laughed too. "And to think that we've shot down five poor innocents."

We agreed that under the circumstances we would not send in any claims nor expect any kudos for our empty victory. We did not tell the others, but that evening at dinner Zulu initiated a new habit in the mess.

"Mick!" he called across the table.

"Yes?" Mick replied.

"I'm ashamed of you!"

A little later, keeping the ball rolling for the mystification of the others, Mick called out to me. "Mac! — you're a cold-blooded murderer!"

The whole squadron was working hard except for a few days on which thunder showers made flying impossible. On one of these, the irrepressible Steve Godfrey, having a roving commission and being free from the restrictions of 'orders', returning from a 'strafe' almost on his last pint of petrol, was caught in a thunderstorm. He could not afford to climb above it, and the deluge forced him closer and closer to the ground till he finally crashed. Onlookers declared that his machine had been hit by lightning, but Steve stoutly denied this. His injuries were purely superficial, a cut face and lacerated arm and leg.

When we crashed it almost invariably happened that we were thrown forward in the cockpit and our faces came into violent contact with the windscreen — resulting in superficial cuts which frequently demanded stitching, and because of which we were required to have injections of anti-tetanus serum. At times the dining-table resembled a training camp for bruisers, and when Steve's face was adorned with criss-crosses of plaster Zulu declared we resembled a nest of brigands.

In the anteroom, Mick, feeling more at his ease with the others, produced a violin and, as a relief to the gramophone records of which we were all tiring, often played his favourites. Kreisler's 'Caprice Viennois' and Schubert's 'Ave Maria'. Beethoven's 'Seventh Symphony' and Schubert's 'Unfinished' were forgotten whenever Mannock took his violin from its case.

The subdued but optimistic spirit that resulted from so much aerial activity and our musical evenings contributed to the camaraderie between the pilots. We had many valiant and reliable scrappers, Keen, Zulu, Godfrey, Hall, Tudhope, Crole, Pettigrew, while the more junior members, Barlow, Kennedy, Harrison, Wallwork, Usher and P. W. Smith, were showing signs of becoming fighters. Talk of fellows who stayed out of scraps had ceased to worry us, and the return of the good old Padre after a three weeks' sojourn with another squadron held the mess together as a place of repose and peace.

Major Tilney's ambition to make our small camp an 'ideal home' made him add one essential, a bathhouse with a cold spray. Previously we had used the baths provided for the miners on the pit-head, a concession I managed to get from the manager, the friendly Monsieur Vignat. Our spray caused considerable amusement among troops passing along the road, for occasionally four of us, clad only in towels wrapped like kilts around our waists, were to be seen playing tennis and diving periodically into the hut to emerge dripping wet for another game. Mick never indulged in tennis, and the sight of him lying back in a deckchair, completely relaxed and snoring away discordantly, often resulted in a rude and watery awakening. He seemed to be able to sleep in any din, either up at Mazingarbe or at the side of the noisy tennis court. This capacity for relaxing was possibly very much to his advantage. His enthusiasm and driving force could never have been sustained had he continued to 'live' at the pitch he did when over the lines.

A rainy day was usually an excuse for varying our excitement by crowding into a tender and the Squadron car and departing to Amiens, where we had several jovial 'parties'. These trips were a relief, and it was unfortunate that one flight had to remain in Bruay in case the clearing of the weather necessitated a patrol.

Events began moving on our front in the first days of August. The Canadians had made only one sally since the battle on Vimy Ridge, and, having consolidated the large sector already captured, it was arranged that the remaining important strategic points on the front should be attacked. When an event was pending it was the custom to let fresh divisions replace the troops that had been holding the line, the tired infantry retiring to the support line. The usual method of changing divisions was by the gradual process of bringing the troops up to the line and relieving each battalion one by one. Owing to the danger of being watched by the enemy either through observers in aircraft or balloons the operation had to be carried out under cover of darkness, a slow and inconvenient process.

According to what we heard, the Canadians preferred changing their troops during daylight and, as absolute secrecy was essential, the R.F.C. was entrusted with the task of blinding the enemy to the unusual movements of the troops.

On two occasions before my arrival '40' had successfully brought down all the balloons on their sector of the front, allowing the divisions to be replaced unknown to the enemy. Bond, Lemon, McKenzie, Walder, Morgan and Thompson had performed the first feat of flying over the trenches at fifty feet from the ground, right to the German balloons three or four miles on the other side of the lines, where they had sent them all down in flames. All the pilots had returned with their machines riddled with bullet holes, but the scheme had been so successful that in early May another attempt was made. This time, Mannock, Hall, Cudemore, Redler, Parry and Captain Nixon went over, Nixon failing to get back. The balloons were destroyed, but Mannock was the only one to arrive at the aerodrome, and his Nieuport had been so seriously damaged by bullets that it had to be 'written off'. The others had had their tanks pierced, their controls damaged, or their engines disabled.

No pilot was ever expected to undertake a second 'balloon strafe', the work being done by the junior members of the Squadron. There had been much chaffing about these 'strafes', and as the possibility of another becoming necessary made it probable that each new batch of pilots would have to undertake it, the prospect hung like a cloud over every junior fighter. The real dangers were never discussed and the 'strafes' were surrounded with an ominous secrecy which induced the experienced pilots to reproach the more boisterous youths by saying, "What you need is a 'balloon strafe' to knock the stuffing out of you." Participation in one was regarded as a baptism.

On the evening of the 8th August the atmosphere at dinner was constrained and excited, and on retiring to my hut Mick and Hall joined me.

Mick stood leaning against the doorpost and grinned jeeringly at me. "You're for the high jump tomorrow."

"How?" I asked, wondering what escapade of mine had by some chance come to the ears of the CO.

Each glanced at the other significantly.

"That's right, isn't it, Hall?" Mick said, to prolong my suspense.

"What the devil do you mean?" I demanded.

"It's quite true, Mac," Hall said. "There's a *balloon strafe* to-morrow."

They came into the hut and sat on Hall's bed, telling me what a 'strafe' involved.

We had to cross the trenches, flying as close to the ground as possible; 'contour-chase' up to the balloon that had been allotted to us; and finally send it down in flames before returning on a similar journey back to our side. The contour-chasing at from ten to twenty feet from the ground made it more difficult for the enemy machine-gunners to get their sights on us as, at that height, our speed appeared to be much greater than if we flew at two or three hundred feet.

The orders seemed very simple, but as the trenches were occupied by Germans with rifles, machine-gun emplacements, each with four or five machine-guns, and the balloons were protected by machine-guns and 'flaming onion' batteries, the simplicity part of it proved to be an illusion.

I was very grateful for Mick's and Hall's advice.

"Keep as close to the ground as possible, five or six feet if you can."

"Don't get rattled and fire at a machine-gun emplacement that peppers you."

"When you get to the balloon, have a good look round to see where the flaming onion battery is," and, "For God's sake mind the telephone wires, they're all over the place, both on their side and ours."

Hall told me that the news was not to be imparted to the others until the next morning, as thoughts of what they would have to face might disturb their sleep.

"We know you're all right," Hall said. "It would be mean of us not to tell you."

"It won't worry old Mac," Mick added, and to me, "I promise I'll count every bullet hole when you get back."

Hall departed to join a game of poker in the mess, and Mick decided that we might as well have a drink together at 'Odette's'. The balloon strafe seemed to worry him more than it did me for, on returning to the camp, having said nothing about it till then, he whispered, "You'll be all right."

The next morning the whole squadron congregated at Mazingarbe. Kennedy, Harrison, Pettigrew, Tudhope, Herbert and I were to 'go over the top', and the others gathered round to see us off.

The whole affair seemed to have been better organised than on previous occasions, and a certain measure of safety was offered to us by the artillery. The batteries were to bombard the front line and support trenches so as to keep the Germans in their dugouts, leaving intervals of two hundred yards through which we could fly.

Zero hour was 9 a.m., and the barrage was due to start at 8.50 and finish at 9.5. We were given the option of flying through the 'safety lanes' or of waiting until 9.6 when every gun would have ceased firing.

I had a horror of meeting a shell in the air or of flying into a column of soil thrown up by an exploding shell, this latter having nearly brought me down a fortnight before; so I elected to wait until the barrage was lifted.

The others chose the 'safety lanes and after they left I had several more minutes' chaff from Mick, Hall and Godfrey. We were within sight of the trenches and could see the earth being hurled into the air by our shells as the five machines quickly wended their way to the balloons.

Then Major Tilney shouted, "Barrage is up, Mac!" and with a final nod to Mick I took off.

We had each been allotted a balloon, mine being the southernmost one, while Herbert's was at the north end. As my machine rose into the air Herbert's balloon went down in a long column of flame and smoke — an encouraging sight.

There was no climbing to do, and as the clover field was so near the trenches I was over the latter within a minute, catching sight here and there of upturned faces on which the sun was shining. My machine was only nine or ten feet above them when it seemed to me that my lonely Nieuport suddenly became the target for every machine-gun on the front, short bursts, staccato firing and continuous determined shooting. I imagined every Fritz in the trenches grabbing for his rifle, and actually saw one or two firing at me. With no conscious volition on my part I began 'crazy flying first on one wing-tip then on the other, squirming and dodging to escape the hail of bullets that were being fired, yet all the time keeping a wary eye open for telephone lines.

They were really breathless moments, for any stray shot might have hit my machine and, flying at that height, I should have had no chance to land properly. But as long as I continued to twist and turn, refusing to fly straight for more than a second, no one could have a fair chance to get his sights on me. The main danger lay in flying too high or in remaining in line with a machine-gun battery sufficiently long to let them fire along my line of flight.

To my intense relief my engine was growling away savagely, and after only half a minute of severe firing the shots tailed off and finally ceased. Flying low and hopping over the crude telephone cables for over a mile, I found myself above green fields. There was a village ahead and, curious to see what it was like, I flew directly over the housetops. The street had a peaceful countrified appearance and a few surprised German soldiers and peasants stared up at me. The sight of my red, white and blue circles made one soldier drop a bucket he was carrying, to dash for cover — or to fetch a rifle.

Soon afterwards I saw another Nieuport — Harrison's. He was flying at right angles to my course, apparently 'lost'. His balloon was still up. On looking towards the east I saw to my chagrin that there was an extra balloon, south of the others, about two hundred feet from the ground. Signing to Harrie to take his own one I made tracks for mine.

As I flew at forty or fifty feet from the ground, three or four miles behind the German lines, a feeling of great serenity came over me. The balloon had been suspended at about four thousand feet, but the Germans were pulling it down with all speed — only to make my job easier. On reaching it, however, it was still at fifteen hundred feet and, feeling quite confident, I made up my mind to wait until they had pulled it down to two or three hundred feet. Passing close to it I could see a redoubt on either side of the winch, probably containing the machine-gun and 'onion' batteries. It was then a good idea came to me. The two batteries were to the west of the balloon, and if I attacked from the east they would not be able to fire at me for fear of hitting the gas-bag themselves. With this in view I flew over a mile to the east of them where I saw a column of Germans approaching along a road, led by a long troop of mounted officers. Possibly because the last thing they expected to see was a British machine flying low down so far behind their lines, they made no attempt to scatter to the side of the road.

Undecided what to do, I zoomed up to three or four hundred feet and, in a spirit of devilment, dived hell-for-leather at the leaders.

The sight of a friendly machine diving with full engine is disconcerting enough, but the sight of my hostile circles must have caused consternation amongst the Germans. The horses stampeded, and on circling round I saw several of them, riderless, tearing across the adjoining fields. The men and officers were sprawling across the road in ridiculous attitudes into which they had thrown themselves to escape my wheels.

The balloon was nearly down by this time so, flying straight for it, I took careful aim at a light blotch on the greenish-grey fabric. I had thought out carefully how best to set the gas alight, by aiming fairly high up on the 'sausage' and making sure that my bullets all went in at the same place. The last bullets would then ignite the gas escaping from the punctures caused by the first shots. We used Buckingham ammunition for this work, and as it was the first time I had fired it I was fascinated by the sight of the smoke streamers entering the fabric. After firing less than half a drum I had to turn aside to avoid crashing into the balloon. Immediately I was clear of the unshapely mass there was a 'woof' below me and hundreds of flaming tongues of fire dithered into the air all round me — flaming onions. The result of the Buckingham on the balloon was an anti-climax. I had expected to see smoke and huge flames, instead of which, nothing happened.

Flying east to get room to make another attempt, I attacked even more determinedly, this time holding my fire till within a hundred yards of the balloon. Again nothing happened, and as the drum was almost finished I had to retire to change it. At the height I was flying this would have been impossible, but by carefully manipulating the joy-stick I succeeded at two hundred feet. In my haste to get on with the work and being afraid to glance downward to place the empty drum in its proper holder, I threw it overboard, hoping that it would deal a knock-out to one of the Germans who, by this time, had picked themselves up.

On my third effort the balloon began to look rather limp, and having emptied another half-drum into it (my third drum was filled with ordinary ammunition) I remembered the second balloon. If the stunt were to be successful that too had to be destroyed, or at least disabled. The first was completely *hors de combat*, smoke was issuing from the end I had used as target, and the whole unsightly mass was collapsing rapidly. I had hoped for fire, instead there was only smoke. On heading south for the other balloon the 'onion' battery had another shot at me. Although the brilliant fire balls seemed to spring up all round, none of them hit my machine.

The Germans had left the second balloon at two hundred feet, and braving machine-gun attack I fired the remainder of my second drum into the eastern side of it. Again nothing happened but as the fabric must have had forty or fifty punctures the balloon could not possibly go up again that day.

Having achieved my purpose, even without the spectacular effect of a balloon in flames, I headed for the lines, still with the same feeling of cheerfulness. I had then been about twenty-five minutes on the German side, and the sight of Herbert's balloon must have put any low-flying scouts on the qui vive so, glancing anxiously behind and above me, I tore across the countryside only twenty or thirty feet from the ground. The excitement, and flying so close to the ground made me so hot that, despite the danger of letting go the throttle, I took off my flying cap and opened my coat.

Approaching the clear-cut Hindenburg-Drocourt line I saw two khaki-clad figures standing on the parapet — poor devils, they were prisoners. Seeing my British markings they waved enthusiastically.

Just ahead, where a long, barren, shell-blasted ridge ran parallel to the front line, the soil was being thrown up into the air in a vicious bombardment by our artillery.

The weakness of the Canadians during the changeover necessitated a constant barrage being maintained to keep the Germans down in their trenches, This one was not a safety measure, there were no lanes, so, literally soaking in perspiration, I turned south to reach the quieter front opposite the Australians. Everything seemed so hot I was afraid my overheated engine would seize, and I expected to hear the clanking that would tell me a piston had broken.

At length I reached the marshland near the Scarpe, and after flying over the German trenches to the accompaniment of still more machine-gun fire I eventually recognised our own khaki uniforms in the trenches. Everyone I saw on our side of the lines was waving.

The others had been back some time when I reached Bruay. Every machine had returned, and there was great excitement. Several red-hatted staff officers were on the aerodrome, and when it was confirmed that all the balloons were down we repaired to the mess to have a proper breakfast.

On the way Mick overtook us. "What do you think!" he said, pointing an accusing finger at me, "that blighter's only got one bullet hole in his machine — in the tail plane."

Several of the others had had an exciting time; Harrie's machine was riddled, Herbert's and Pettigrew's were also damaged, Kennedy's had bullet holes in every section of it except the tank (and the pilot), while Tud, as usual, had had the worst of it. He had flown into a German telephone cable and, miraculously, had wound many yards of it round his propeller without any worse damage than a split in one of the blades. Not contented with strafing their balloons, both Tud and George Pettigrew had carried the war properly into the enemy's country by 'shooting up' troops on the ground. Tud had seen a crowd of Germans sitting round a pond and, on opening fire on them, saw them diving hurriedly into the water to take cover. 'George' had spotted a company of cyclists riding along a road several miles behind the lines and had scattered them with a burst from his machine-gun.

The staff fellows questioned me closely about my inability to set the balloons alight, one of them stoutly declaring that the balloons must have been filled with helium and not with hydrogen. The newly discovered helium gas was non-inflammable, but we afterwards discovered that the Germans had never used it. My failure had been caused by bad marksmanship or bad luck.

The staff interest in the occasion was not mere curiosity in the unique method of changing divisions. Throughout July, the Fifth Army had been attacking on the Ypres front and, to persuade the Germans that all our forces had not been concentrated in the battle area, army 'headquarters' considered it advisable to provide a 'divertisement' on another sector of the line. In their advance the Canadians had stopped short of Lens and several important woods or copses on the western side of the town. In addition an important vantage-point, the famous 'Hill 70', was still held by the Germans, so that no more profitable objective for a minor attack could have been found.

Before the beginning of the Ypres battle we had seen columns of artillery passing the aerodrome with all types of guns from three-inch to twelve-inch howitzers. Hour after hour and day after day the heavy camouflaged guns, accompanied by all types of motor and mule transport, had wended their way over the hilly roads south of Houdain on the route from the Somme to Bailleul and the intended battle area.

For the small attack on Lens there appeared to be no preparation behind the immediate front, but at Mazingarbe there was some little indication of movement and suspense. Canadian Colonels and even Brigadier-Generals developed the habit of coming to the clover field to have long talks with us about the position on the German side: "How were they holding the line?" "Could we co-operate with the ground troops?" "What was the best way of shooting down hostile trench-strafing machines?"

Mick and I offered to spend a few days in the front line teaching the machine-gunners how to fire at enemy aircraft. After the experiences we had had, the destroying of a D.F.W. or Albatros from the ground should have been an easy matter, but our proposition was contemptuously refused.

Several more batteries were planted in front of us, and the arrival of one of these caused me some amusement. I was sitting in the clover watching the eastern horizon for signs of German machines or the white puff balls of our Archie that would tell me of their approach, when my eyes lit on a small thicket of trees that was unfamiliar. It was only three hundred yards from the edge of the field, and I felt sure that I must have seen it before. Some of the trees were green while others wore the brown tint of autumn. On glancing at it again several minutes later, I noticed that it had changed its position, and considering such an unnatural phenomenon worthy of investigation I walked over to see what was happening.

About twenty small trucks were standing on a narrow-gauge railway, each truck garlanded as if it were a Christmas tree with all sorts and sizes of branches. Amidst and underneath this 'thicket' were several guns with their complement of gunners and shells. The gunners were sitting astride the shells; six-or seven-inchers, as far as I could see, and as I approached the stationary cavalcade so appropriately and naturally camouflaged, a sergeant called out: "Do you mind putting your cigarette out, Sir!" The battery was in charge of a youthful officer who was going up the line for the first time. He was nervous, and as Bully-Grenay was receiving a little more than its usual 'hate' he glanced apprehensively in that direction while speaking to me.

"Why are you walking about here, you'll give us away!" he said from underneath a panoply of fresh branches.

He told me his orders were to smuggle his battery to a brick works west of Grenay, and that he had to take every precaution against observation by the enemy. He chided me for 'dangerously' walking about in full view of the enemy, and not even my pointing out that our bright aluminium Nieuports were standing in a field only a few hundred yards away could quieten him. The bombardment of Bully-Grenay and the tangled mass of rusted barbed wire covering a disused communication trench on our right convinced him that we were within the 'battle area'. Even the expostulations of his sergeant, an old experienced veteran, failed to persuade him that there was no great danger. It was not so much the quite justifiable precautions he was taking as his attitude towards me that tempted me to indulge in a bit of 'leg-pulling'.

"The only danger here," I said, "is the Observation Post on Hill 70 at Loos. They can see us, but if you go on moving as fast as you have done, they're bound to spot a clump of trees that walks about." An hour later I noticed that they had not moved more than a hundred yards. He reached his position safely that night, but before a week had passed I heard that the Germans had registered a direct hit on the store of over a hundred shells which the officer had had stacked right between the guns. Nothing could be found either of the guns or the personnel: their remains had been scattered over the already bloody waste that stretched in front of our clover field.

When preparations were finished, 'Stand by' sounded for us on the afternoon of the 14th August. Our orders were to the effect that except for one evening patrol, no machines were to leave the ground and that all machines had to be ready for the morrow.

After dinner, Major Tilney took the senior pilots into the orderly room and gave us our orders. One flight was to carry out low-flying defence, using Mazingarbe as headquarters, while the other two flights were to operate from Bruay and to patrol behind the German lines at different heights to prevent any enemy flights approaching the centre of the battle. No. 43 Squadron, our companion squadron at Auchel, was to perform the disagreeable duty of 'contact patrol' for our advancing troops, and to 'harass the enemy communications'. The low-flying flight of Nieuports was to protect 43 Squadron's obsolete Sopwith two-seaters against the attack of any hostile fighters which might escape our notice. To assist the defending flight it was decided that Mick should operate as a freelance with a roving commission for the day while I was to take charge of the flight arrangements.

The principal objectives for the Canadians were: Hill 70 (Loos), Bois Hugo, Bois Rasé, and in addition Cite St. Elisabeth, on the outskirts of Lens. We had hoped that the complete capture of the town would take place, and Mick, Tud, Ken and I had already arranged which estaminet we would frequent when it was captured.

On the morning of the 15th the sun shone down on the pitiful countryside west of Lens, on the deserted town, and on the fresh green fields to the east of the battle area. Lens itself was exactly as it had been two months earlier, almost untouched by the war.

There was no enemy activity in the air above twelve thousand feet, and even on descending to eight thousand, where we were pestered by Archie, we failed to find any fighters. At that height the dark khaki-green Sopwith two-seaters were invisible, but we caught sight of several of our more conspicuous Nieuports. There a good deal of shelling to the west and north-west of Lens, but the town itself was left severely alone even until lunch, by which time we had 'put in' two patrols.

At two o'clock we heard that for the remainder of the day pilots could patrol 'at their own discretion', a piece of news which seemed encouraging. For fear of missing any of the excitement I spent an hour circling between five and six thousand feet on the east side of Lens. What a difference there was in the appearance of the town! The clean fresh country look had gone and a cloud of red-brick dust hung like a pall over both sides of it, almost blotting out the streets and houses. Apparently both the Germans and ourselves were shelling it, and as I was returning fairly low to land at Mazingarbe, a mine or a German ammunition dump blew up, throwing a column of debris almost as high as my machine. It must have been hell for the troops fighting down there, in the heat, the dust, and with the shells from both sides landing amongst them. The brilliant sun shone down on it ironically.

When I landed at Mazingarbe it was as if I had been transported to another world, into a peaceful garden fete. The bright-coloured Nieuports and the prominent red, white and blue circles on the Sopwiths, combined with the fact that two marquees had been erected and fellows were standing about drinking tea, completed the illusion. The field, recently mown, sent up the sweet smell of clover which brought England very vividly to my mind.

The Sopwiths had experienced a hard time. Two of their machines were missing, and as we stood there talking, another one landed, but instead of taxi-ing in remained in the middle of the aerodrome. The observer stood up, calling, "Ambulance."

We discovered later that the pilot had been wounded by a shot from the ground, and only by an heroic effort had he been able to return and land his observer safely. The knowledge that the life of another depended on him prompted many of these two-seater pilots to acts of quiet determined bravery that went almost unrecorded. In this case the pilot was unconscious before the ambulance could reach him.

Throughout the day we were filled with admiration for the way in which '43' pilots executed their work, without fuss, excitement, or any sign that anything unusual was happening. Their machines were slow, heavy and obsolete (possibly the reason for their being given the work).

After tea I decided to have another spell over the trenches, and while hunting for my machine, noticed a new type of Nieuport standing beside ours. She looked like a racehorse among a lot of old cab hacks; her fuselage was circular in section and perfectly streamlined; her tail plane was a typical 'fish tail', and as a double Lewis gun was mounted on the plane her whole appearance "was so clean and warlike I remarked to the others:

"What a beauty! Whose is she?"

Steve Godfrey told me that he had just brought her from Candas and that if I liked her I could have her in exchange for mine; double Lewis gun included. It was a sporting offer, and I accepted it on the spot. Godfrey, however, did not intend to take advantage of me.

"You'd better take her up first, and then if you think you can do anything with her you're welcome," he said.

It was peculiar how pilots took sudden likes and dislikes to machines. As soon as I had 'taken off' I knew that I had a winner. At two thousand feet she looped, spun, performed Immelmen turns, and generally behaved like an acrobat. My delight was unbounded.

Just as I was thinking of landing her the mechanics put the 'enemy' sign on the ground, and on looking round I spotted four large machines approaching from the east several thousand feet above me. After climbing as quickly as possible I realised that if I hoped to attack them I would have to do so from underneath.

Although attacking a lone two-seater from this position does not entail any great risk providing the attacker keeps in line with the fuselage, the presence of other machines in which the observers can get a comfortable sight on him makes the manoeuvre a particularly dangerous one. I was already in position and was attempting to sight on the front of the fuselage when I observed that the machine was British.

Annoyed at having gone through the excitement and tension of taking on overwhelming odds, I side-stalled and dived almost to the ground without 'touching' my engine.

My temerity in hoping that I could attack four D.F.W.s from such a position had caused considerable amusement. The machines I had sighted were D.H.4s, our new bombing machines, but as we had never seen them on our front before, there was some excuse for our having made the mistake.

Steve Godfrey confirmed his offer, and to my great joy the 'Silver Queen' was handed over to me officially. Several of us then started off on lone patrols over the German trenches, but except for one venturesome Albatros which Mannock succeeded in bringing down there was no real activity on the part of the enemy. At the end of a strenuous day there was a great deal of hand-shaking with the pilots of '43' before we returned to Bruay.

The celebration that night was subdued. The Canadians had taken the strategical positions on the northern and eastern sides of Lens, the Squadron had brought down five enemy machines (Mannock three); but we were tired and somewhat despondent because of the losses sustained by our companion squadron. They had lost two machines (two pilots and two observers), and two pilots and an observer had been wounded. They had brought down a German two-seater and a scout.

When we were sitting on the tennis court after dinner, listening to the 'Seventh Symphony' in the dark, my mind travelled back over the day. I felt happy. Mick had once more proved his worth, the attack had been successful and — I had the machine of my dreams. With her the German Archie gunners were not likely to trouble me much because of her similarity of outline to that of their own scouts, the double Lewis gun would give me a great moral advantage over the enemy, and I had had a feeling of confidence in her from the moment I had stepped into the cockpit.

This last may not appear so important until it is appreciated that as most of our work was carried on miles behind the

German lines the demoralising effect of having a machine on which one could not rely was considerable. Not only did it mean that in 'scraps' the machine might fail at a crucial moment, as it had done with Mannock many times, but, as landing on the German side of the lines was regarded by their infantry as a capital crime and the unfortunate pilot was likely to meet with summary justice in retaliation for our attacks on their trenches, a weak machine or engine trebled the danger to the pilot.

Some days later there was news of movements of German troops behind the lines, and No. 2 Squadron was ordered to take large-scale photographs of the German communications.

This unpleasant duty demanded that photographs be taken at not more than three thousand feet, and as the railheads were several miles behind the lines the risk of the No. 2 A.W.s being attacked by enemy scouts who would have time to take off was considered so great that the photographic machines were escorted by flights of fighters.

For some reason or other Kennedy was not on duty, and when Mannock was told that we were to accompany a flight of No. 2 Squadron's Armstrong Whitworths, he called Tudhope, Harrison and myself.

"Now's our chance to show 'em. The 'Ack.W.s' will be at two or three thousand feet, and the air's bound to be lousy with Huns. We'll give 'em blazes."

As a flight we had never previously acted as escorts, and ignorant of what the duty might entail we made no prearranged plans.

The rendezvous with the A.W.s was over Hesdigneul aerodrome, where we met the four machines and headed towards the lines. Crossing at six thousand feet we were greeted by a salvo of Archie from all the batteries on the front. Shells exploded above us, below us, and amongst us, but the heavy two-seaters plodded steadily onwards, making no attempt to avoid the bursts or to deceive the gunners. This continued for several minutes until the A.W.s began to lose height in order to get down to their objectives. To the north a flight of enemy scouts appeared, another approached from the south-east. It looked as if Mannock were going to get his chance of 'giving them blazes

With a hurried waggle of his planes he darted off towards the north, followed by Tudhope. This left me in a quandary. As there was a hostile flight in the vicinity it was obviously dangerous to leave the photographic machines; their attention was needed for their work and, from what I had heard, they were not likely to quit, so I decided to stay beside them. Harrison wagged his wings to draw my attention to the German flight that was now closing in on us. The A.W.s began to patrol steadily up and down while the anti-aircraft gunners, having had time to get our range again, bombarded us worse than ever. The shelling probably kept the enemy scouts from descending, for they circled round about a thousand feet above.

Up north there was a mix-up of fighting machines from which one of the Albatros spun down to the ground. 'Archie' slackened, and Harrison pointed frantically to the Germans who were taking up their formation and were preparing to dive. It was apparent that the only way to prevent their reaching the A.W.s was to turn round and engage them in a 'dog-fight' at some distance from the photographic machines.

I pulled down my guns and, signing to Harrison to do the same, turned right about to face the leader of the German flight. This had the desired effect for, after letting him have the first burst and firing a second at another, Harrison following suit, the Germans scattered. When closing in again on the A.W.s there were only three Germans above us and they were now heading east. One of the A.W.s fired a white Very light, evidently a sign that the photography had been completed, and we fell into formation again. Neither Mannock, Tudhope nor the other German flight were in sight as we flew back to the lines.

We escorted the A.W.s to their aerodrome before landing at Bruay where, much to our relief, we found that Mannock and Tudhope had landed safely.

While I was filling in my combat report Mannock came up to me.

"How many did you get?" he asked.

"None that I can be certain about."

"What! and all those Huns about!"

He was furious with me, and disappointed.

"If you had only come with me we would have had the whole blinkin' lot."

"Our job was to protect the A.W.s, not to run off after death and glory," I answered.

Had it not been for the intervention of the C.O. to say that the officer commanding No. 2 Squadron had telephoned to thank the two pilots that had stuck to their escorting duty, Mick and I might have come to blows.

That evening we argued it out when we were alone. The day's work had revealed to us that the unusual duty had been carried out in a haphazard fashion, and that if we were to work amicably and efficiently as a flight it behoved Mick to make plans for *each* patrol. It was only by sheer good luck that the escorting job had been performed successfully. We could not expect to be so fortunate the next time.

CHAPTER VII

BOTH Tudhope and Kennedy had shown us that they were prepared to attack regardless of the consequences to themselves. In concentrating too much on firing at one of the enemy machines, they usually forgot the danger of another hostile fighter's attacking them. Harrison, although undoubtedly a brave and reliable pilot, did not seem to have the same enthusiasm as the others. He managed to come out of 'dog-fights' with a whole machine, but he very rarely fired his gun. By this time we had begun to understand 'Harrie', and Mick often declared: "God help poor old Fritz the day Harrie goes bloodthirsty!" (Mick was right, for early in 1918 Harrie was one of the most aggressive fighters in the Squadron.)

Mick very frequently took Harrie over the lines in the afternoon, 'to rub his nose into a Hun'. After chasing up and down beyond the German lines, Mick would land at Mazingarbe, while Harrie, disgruntled at Mick's eagerness to see him 'blooded', returned to Bruay. Kennedy usually accompanied me.

So it was that on many occasions Mick, Kennedy and I landed at Mazingarbe. On the landing-ground we could do as we pleased, without having to report or even have our 'flying times' taken. We went up when we felt inclined and, a very great consideration, we were able to go into Bethune to tea whenever cream cakes and fresh pastries appealed to our healthy appetites. We had discovered a teashop in a side street near the Officers' Club, a clean, fresh place owned by a dark, very attractive French girl, where we could obtain all the delicacies for which the country is famous. Mademoiselle admired 'Les Officiers Anglais' and, judging by the very reasonable prices she charged, her work must have been more of self-imposed duty than a profit-making business. We nicknamed her the 'Queen of Sheba'.

Because of his knowledge of French, she and Kennedy were soon fast friends and their innocent flirtations over the teacups caused Mick and myself a great deal of amusement. Mick's capacity for enjoying French pastries was only limited by his desire to get back to the landing-ground. As long as he forgot the war and the Germans that might be prowling about the lines, he would sit quietly demolishing cakes; but immediately the memory of the clover field returned, he would jump up and demand the bill, and we would hurry back to Mazingarbe. These teas at 'The Queen of Sheba's' formed a very pleasant background to our work.

On the landing-ground we took turns at patrolling up and down over the trenches, between four thousand and eight thousand feet, keeping a look out for enemy two-seaters and occasionally looking towards the clover field to see if the others had put out a signal. On the ground Mick proved to be incorrigibly lazy. He would lie for an hour, flat on his stomach, watching the eastern sky with his searching blue eyes and kicking his heels in the air. I was with him one afternoon while he was reposing like this: we were both watching the clouds of bricks and dust that were being hurled into the air in Bully-Grenay. The bombardment was particularly severe even for Bully, and when the firing subsided I remarked that it would be interesting to see how much extra damage had been done by such a 'strafe'.

"Come on then," Mick said, jumping up immediately, "I've heard there's a teashop. Let's explore it! Come on, Ken."

We found the main street still smelling of explosive. Dust hung over everything, and the sight of the ruined houses, of which only a few gables were standing, brought back with full bitterness the sufferings of the countryside around us. The place was deserted, but half-way along the street on the left-hand side the skeletons of one or two remained, merely crumbling walls; outside one was a notice: 'TEA-ROOM', written in chalk on a piece of trench boarding. True enough, on descending to the cellar we found a cosy room with wicker chairs and wooden tables. There were two girls there, plucky French girls, determined to withstand the bombardments as long as they were allowed to remain in their 'house'. Mick, with typical optimism, asked for cream cakes.

"But it is impossible, Monsieur. We are not in a big town. As you see, there are no shops here," one of the girls said. Very apologetically Ken asked what we could obtain.

"I can make Monsieurs some fresh scones. We have a little flour left."

While we were waiting for the scones a grimy Canadian Corporal climbed down the stairs.

"What do you guys want here? We're supposed to keep out of it except in the mornings."

"That's all right, bo'," Mick replied. "We've come over from the landing-ground; going back soon."

The Canadian looked at Mick's shoulder-straps. "You take my tip then, Cap', an' beat it as quick as you can before the 'x-y-z.s' start again."

We finished our teas as quickly as we could. Being stuck in Bully-Grenay during a bombardment would not have been pleasant.

Before we reached the landing-ground the Germans had recommenced their hymn of hate and, in memory and honour of the indomitable French girls, we set off on a really aggressive patrol. For lack of anything better to shoot I attacked another balloon and fired into the German trenches on the way back.

It was still early when I recrossed the lines and, hoping Mick would see my machine in Mazingarbe, landed there instead of returning to the home aerodrome.

I was lying in the thick clover keeping a look out when Mick's machine appeared, gliding towards the ground. His landing was much too fast, and to my amazement he ran straight into the haystack at the end of the field. I was ready to laugh at the sight of an 'old' pilot like Mannock failing to steer clear of a haystack, but, seeing him staggering from the machine holding both hands over his face, I ran over to him. He was trembling as I put my hand over his shoulder.

"Good heavens, Mick! What a damned silly thing to do," was my way of expressing the sympathy I felt. "Didn't you see the haystack?"

He stood silent for a minute, then took his hands from his face and blinked.

"No, that's the tragedy of it, old boy, I didn't see it. I can't see on that side; but it's all right, I can still see with my other one. I thought *that* was done in."

As usual his face had been brought into violent contact with the windscreen. The flesh round one eye was beginning to darken, but when he caught sight of his machine his face broadened into a rueful smile. The snub-nosed Nieuport engine was half-embedded in the haystack, the upper part of which had been pushed over by the force of the impact. It appeared almost as if the Nieuport were trying to eat the hay. Mannock then told me that at ten thousand feet, six or seven miles on the enemy side of the lines, his engine had 'cut out' completely, forcing him to glide all the way back. Fortunately the German two-seaters he had hoped to meet had not come his way.

On the 21st Kennedy and I spent all our free time at Mazingarbe watching and waiting for signs of aerial activity on the German side, but as nothing exciting happened we adjourned to the tea-room at Bully-Grenay and then returned to Bruay just before dark. To our annoyance we learnt that it was our turn for dawn patrol on 'trench strafing' duty. We had no time for a meal, and knowing that there was nothing but tinned lobster to eat at the landing-ground I asked one of the A.M.s to fetch some eggs. While waiting for these, I told Kennedy to take off a few minutes before me because of the difficulty I would have in seeing his machine in the dim light.

When Sergeant Smart handed me the eggs he offered to bet me that some, if not all of them, would be broken during my landing. While the mechanics were 'sucking in' the engine, I could hear him whistling 'Scrambled eggs in the new-mown hay' from 'You ought to see my home in Dixie'.

Both Kennedy and I landed safely and, instead of the dinner we had missed, took the next best thing — egg mixed with whisky and condensed milk. Our mechanics warned us that we had better retire to bed as we had to be up so early, but Kennedy was restless and had no desire to sleep. He opened the portable gramophone and put on a record of a song which evidently appealed to him, for he played it over several times, humming the refrain and insisting that I should memorise the words …

I shall see you to-night, Love,
In our beautiful dreamland,
And your eyes will be bright, Dear,
With the love-light that gleams for me.
To my heart I will press you,
I will kiss and caress you,
So good-night and God bless you,
I shall see you to-night.

I have neither heard nor seen the words of the song since, but so vivid is my memory of that night that I have written them down just as Kennedy sang them.

At last he put the record away, and a 'monitory' snore from the mechanics' tent reminded us that our fitters and riggers had to be up very early to prepare the machines for the patrol. Kennedy was silent for a few minutes, thoughtfully puffing his cigarette and sipping his drink. The stillness of the night was broken by spasmodic bursts of artillery fire — the Germans shelling Bully-Grenay, and the answering roar of our own twelve-inch howitzer. Until we could get accustomed to the noise sleep was impossible.

During a lull Kennedy turned to me: "Do you believe in hunches, Mac?"

I did not understand what he meant by 'hunch' until he explained that it was American slang for a premonition.

"I've got a powerful hunch," he said, "I shall never see my girl again — I'll never last out another day." Then he told me of his university life in Toronto, of his home life and of his fiancée. In conclusion he added: "And in another twenty-four hours, Mac, it'll be all over. What was the use of it?"

Kennedy was my age — twenty-one, and it was strange to hear him talking in this despondent way. I thought of Mannock's premonition; but somehow Ken was different. I hated this talk of 'finishing'.

110

I told him the depressing effect of the shelling and the sentimental reminder of the song had encouraged his morbid thoughts, and advised him to try to sleep.

To my relief the next morning I saw him returning safe from the first patrol. The dawn 'strafe' had to be carried out in such a poor light that we were forced to descend very low in order to recognise the colour of the uniforms in the trenches before firing at the troops, and at that height we formed easy targets for any intelligent machine-gunner.

After a breakfast of scrambled eggs we set out on another patrol and, my mind still influenced by Kennedy's conversation on the previous night, I made him accompany me instead of allowing him to go off alone.

On returning safely once more to Bruay, and after another breakfast, this time in comfort, Kennedy, to make up for his sleepless night, retired to bed.

The exhilarating effect of the morning's flying had made me keen to go over the lines again, and as the remainder of the flight — Mannock, Tudhope and Harrison — were due for patrol, I offered to go with them. Mannock refused, reminding me that I was not permitted to take three official patrols in such quick succession, but that if I cared to go up the line on my own initiative I could act as 'fairy godfather' to them.

This particular morning we were given ample opportunity of practising our strategy, for on joining the other three over the lines, I saw an enemy flight of seven machines beneath them, and, a little way to the east, another flight of five above them. Throughout an entire patrol from the Scarpe to La Bassée, the Germans maintained the same positions relative to Mick's flight. When Mannock climbed to reach the Albatros flight above him, they also climbed, and in this stalemate condition it obviously behoved me to do something to precipitate a 'dog-fight'.

On my attempting to climb above the upper flight they eased off towards the east; and at last, fearing that our patrol might have to return through lack of petrol, I resolved to act as 'decoy'. In order to tempt the Germans to come within easy reach of Mannock I joined the flight and, getting alongside

Mick, signed to him that I was going to fly underneath the Germans. He shook his head impatiently, but when I repeated the manoeuvre he agreed and, as a sign to the others to be prepared, wagged his wings violently.

Well aware that the Germans were not likely to attack an experienced fighter acting as 'decoy' I attempted to 'play the fool', and eventually reached a position underneath the Germans and just a little ahead of them. Mick climbed steadily in preparation for the attack, but for a time the Albatros pilots showed no desire to descend on my machine. Ignoring my presence, they continued their course until, having 'eased off' nearly a mile from Mannock, I headed north-west as if to rejoin the flight. Even then they appeared loath to attack me properly, only putting their noses down gently and firing short bursts from their machine-guns.

Much to my relief I noticed that their ammunition was exploding two or three hundred feet behind me. Both tracer and incendiary ammunition are deceptive in this respect, the user is under the impression that his shots are hitting the target as long as they are in direct line with it, while, actually, the bullets may be exploding some distance away. An experiment with von Bartrap's ammunition had shown me that the German incendiary bullets were 'spent' at about one hundred and fifty yards; consequently I was in no imminent danger so long as I kept outside that distance from the leading enemy machine. The actual risk lay in their using ordinary rounds mixed with the incendiary.

Appreciating their mistake, the leader, on his next essay, forced me to side-slip violently in an effort to escape his 'streamers'. This gave me my opportunity. As the attacker pulled out of his 'dive', still above my level, I let down my Lewis guns and, making a complete circle, fired fifteen or twenty rounds at him. Having no sights, and being dependent on tracer bullets to estimate the direction of my bursts, I missed him, but, probably disliking the terrifying sound of the two Lewis guns firing simultaneously, he immediately turned east and was followed closely by the other four. Meanwhile Mannock had also turned east, intent on attacking them, but as they and the seven machines underneath got away without attacking us or giving us the opportunity to engage them, we withdrew.

Mick was waiting for me when I arrived at Bruay. "Look here, young Mac," he said, "I don't want any more of those D.S.O. stunts from you. If anyone is going to get the D.S.O. in this flight, *I* am. My heart was in my mouth the whole time those Huns were firing at you; your machine must be darned well riddled."

From his position in the air it had naturally appeared as if the German bullets had been going through my planes, but on examination we found that none of them had hit my machine.

"Well," Mick remarked, "all I can say is that they will *never* kill you!"

When I told him that I had tried to entice them to a descent on me by feigning to be a new pilot and a fool, he laughed.

"You fathead! you forget the streamer on your tail. They weren't going to give you the chance of getting at them."

I was carrying the single streamer of the 'second-in-command'.

During our instruction and, in fact, throughout our early days, it was considered almost suicidal to let a German machine get into a position above us. The German scouts could only fire forward, two-seaters could fire forward, sideways and backward; but neither of them could aim their guns upwards. With Steve Godfrey's mounting I had the advantage of being able to hit the enemy when he least expected it, that is, from underneath. For this reason I was never afraid of flying under an enemy scout or two-seater. Having proved the efficacy of these tactics, I continued to employ them whenever opportunity arose. The moral effect on the Germans must have been considerable when, added to this surprise, was the speed at which my double Lewis guns fired in contrast to the slow tat-tat-tat of their guns synchronised to fire through the propeller.

It had been a disappointing morning, and after lunch, having had only four hours' sleep the previous night, I retired to bed and did not wake up until six o'clock.

There was no evening patrol for the Squadron and, feeling refreshed, I washed and changed in preparation for an excursion into Bethune after dinner.

In the mess I found Mannock and Padre Keymer indulging in one of their usual arguments. The Wing had lost several young pilots, and our brave old Padre was in a despondent mood. His kindly courageous soul rebelled at the deaths of so many decent young fellows and he was expressing a desire to join the fighting forces himself. Mannock was opposing him: "My dear Padre, there are enough of us here to do the fighting. We've got 'em so well under we have to go over to their side to dig 'em out … and we can keep them there. We need the influence of men like you, particularly on the younger fellows. Yours is really a greater work than fighting and — with all due respect to your courage and your spirit — how old are you? How do you think you would fare as a fighting pilot?"

I had often heard them arguing in this strain, for every time the Padre heard of the death of one of his protégés his bitterness welled over.

Knowing that the argument would only finish by Mick's attacking the Padre on religious grounds, and threatening to 'defrock' him, I went over to the piano, just behind Mick, opened the cover quietly and struck a sharp chord.

"God Almighty," Mannock jumped up. "I'll — I'll ——"

He glared at me and then at the Padre.

"Excuse me, Padre," he said apologetically, "that wasn't blasphemy, it was a real prayer. There's Mac playing that confounded thing — and Kennedy did it the other night. Why doesn't Tilney give it away or blow it up?" He turned to me. "You needn't laugh. I don't want to lose the lot of you."

I remembered what Kennedy had told me.

"Did Ken play it?" I asked.

Mick nodded.

"He accompanied Mick until we stopped him. I'm not superstitious," observed the Padre, "but there certainly seems to be something sinister about that piano. You knew it — then why did *you* touch it?"

"Yes I know, but — it's really queer. Last night Ken and I were sleeping at Mazingarbe and he told me he had a 'hunch' that he wouldn't last more than twenty-four hours."

They were both very serious, and as nothing depressed me more than 'sentiment' and superstition I turned round and struck a few more chords on the piano.

Mannock came over threateningly. "If you don't stop that I'll knock"

"Shut up, you two," the Padre broke in abruptly, and we noticed that Kennedy, followed by several of the others, was entering the mess.

As it was such a lovely evening everyone had changed into slacks.

"What about a drink, Mac?" someone asked, and as I was in charge of the bar I retired to mix cocktails, and was followed by Kennedy.

Silently he watched me measuring the ingredients, then, when I was pouring out the drinks, he said quietly:

"Thank God it's all over for to-day, Mac. I haven't been able to get that feeling out of my mind."

I told him I was glad. He was a close friend, and as the subject was distasteful I gave him one tray of drinks and followed him into the mess with another.

We were helping ourselves when Major Tilney hurried into the mess.

"Blast them!" he burst out. "Some fool of an observer has reported that Dorignies aerodrome is deserted, and we've got to corroborate the report to-night."

As a C.O. Major Tilney was considerate. We were tired.

He looked round the mess, and continued: "It's a dirty job — as if it matters whether we find out to-night or to-morrow morning. I've tried to put it off, but they say they must know before dark — looks like a job for you, Mac. You know those aerodromes round Douai."

"All right, Sir," I replied. "Let's have our drinks first."

Mick expostulated. "But look here, Major, Dorignies is just behind Douai; we can't let Mac go over there alone at this time; all the low-flying Huns will be after him. What about an escort?" and without waiting to hear what the C.O. had to say he turned round to the others: "Who'll come? It'll be a d——d fine lark."

Hall jumped up. "That's the idea. Let's be in it."

Steve Godfrey, Crole, Pettigrew and Harrison acquiesced, but Major Tilney remonstrated.

"Look here, Mick, we'll leave it to Mac. Would you rather go alone or with an escort?" he asked me.

"Alone," I replied.

Both Mannock and Hall insisted that it was unfair to put the question in that way, as I could only give the one answer, and that, as the pilots from the aerodromes round Douai would have a chance to take off to intercept a low-flying machine, I should have little chance of getting back.

I thought it was making a mountain out of a molehill, but Mick clinched the argument by saying that as I was going anyway it would not matter to me whether or not the rest of the Squadron used me as 'bait'.

"All right then, Major," I agreed. "I'd certainly feel more comfortable with some of our fellows about."

With his usual enthusiasm Mick wanted to take the whole Squadron to raid the German aerodromes, but Tilney wisely decreed that the Flight that was to take the early morning patrol should stay behind. He was thinking of the mechanics, many of whom would probably have to be up all night working on our machines in preparation for the next morning.

We made our plans hurriedly. Mick was to lead the first flight, while the second flight was to follow about a thousand feet above him. I was to 'contour chase' right over to Douai and then, when I had got 'corroboration', to climb up underneath the formation.

Forgetting that the others intended 'getting their height' before crossing the lines, I took off immediately they had assembled over the aerodrome. I wore only a light raincoat and no flying cap, and as a precaution, in case of a forced landing on the German side of the lines, my R.F.C. cap and chequebook were in my pocket.

Flying between ten and twenty feet from the ground I crossed the front line to the east of Vimy, where, to my great relief, the machine-gun fire that met me was not nearly so bad as it had been on the morning of the 'balloon strafe'. There were only about thirty seconds of real firing from the trenches before my machine was skimming over green clover fields. As usually happened, the lull brought a feeling of peace and security — the worst was over and, except for the immaculate Hindenburg-Drocourt trenches, there was little sign of the war beyond two or three miles from the front line. In passing over a peaceful village I could see women moving about in the road, and grey-clad German soldiers standing about in groups.

As I was flying at less than a hundred feet from the ground the Archie gunners could not hit me, even had they been aware of my presence. My risk lay in meeting low-flying scouts or of someone telephoning ahead to the aerodrome. To my relief I did not see any machines until I was approaching Douai, when I spotted five fighters to the north at about five or six thousand feet. Looking round to ascertain Mannock's position I observed a few 'specks' amidst clouds of Archie burst, to the north-west, while to the southwest was another large flight, obviously German, as they were flying towards Douai and were losing height.

On reaching my objective I flew round the aerodrome at two or three hundred feet. Except for a few German soldiers who might have been a guard, there was no sign of 'occupation' by aeroplanes. The hangars were shut up.

The Germans were running to the easternmost hangar and, inwardly debating as to whether or not I should 'spend' ammunition on them or save it for the inevitable 'scrap' that was about to take place, I decided to keep my drums intact and to climb towards the escort.

My machine had reached five thousand feet when Mannock attacked the enemy flight that had been approaching from the south-west and was now directly above me. Within a few seconds the clash took place, of scrapping, fighting, writhing machines. From this frenzied mass one dropped in the unmistakable 'uncontrolled' spin, an Albatros.

Zooming quickly as I let down my double Lewis gun in order to fire up into any of the Germans that got above me, I had almost gained their level when, to my horror, I saw a Nieuport careering downwards in a mad dive, streaks of smoke issuing behind it, while the sun vividly lit up the aluminium-painted fuselage and red, white and blue circles. There was another Albatros above me, circling round feverishly. As I fired a burst from both guns right into the front of the fuselage, the first Archie shells exploded in our midst. The German batteries at the front had got our range and bombarded us, regardless of whether their shells were hitting friend or foe. Added to the anxiety of being shot at by machine-guns were the two more terrifying dangers of meeting an Archie shell, or crashing into another machine.

In the most intense part of the fight my machine passed right across Mick's tail plane, only a few feet above him. I could see his eye was glued to his Aldis sight, aiming at an Albatros, but that inexplicable something that warned seasoned pilots of the proximity of another machine made him turn his head, only to realise in a fraction of a second that mine was a friendly machine. I shall never forget the scared expression on his face as he instinctively cowered.

Turning round into the scrap again, I succeeded in 'getting on to the tail' of another German, but by side-slipping and diving he prevented me from getting my guns to bear on him. After following him down to a thousand feet, I gave up the attempt and, on turning westward, discovered that I was again alone.

In the distance a long trail of Archie bursts indicated the course of the others.

Again I felt lonely. I was hot, tired and disgruntled — I had seen one of our machines going down — was it Kennedy's?

Dreading the sound of more machine-guns, I flew towards the lines, climbing steadily and zig-zagging to mislead the Archie gunners.

On reaching Oppy another Nieuport joined me — Crole's — and we flew home together to our aerodrome at Bruay.

When my machine stopped on the ground Mick ran out.

"Thank God you're safe, old boy! I thought you had gone too."

I asked him who were missing.

"Only Ken," he said mournfully, "I saw him going down."

The remainder of the flights were gathered round the orderly-room, filling in combat reports and arguing.

Godfrey and Hall declared that Mick had given them no chance to close in before he attacked, and that, had he manoeuvred properly, their flight could have headed off the Germans.

Mick rounded on them, saying that the Albatros were losing height and would have got away, and that, if the upper flight had taken advantage of their extra height, they could have been in the thick of the scrap. "And, besides," he added, "it was only a matter of a few seconds before they would have seen Mac. Seven of them. I hold back? Not bloody likely."

Amid the excitement I filled in my combat report accurately stating the condition in which I had found the German aerodrome. Everyone else had forgotten the object of the expedition. We were able to claim several 'victories', but to Mick and myself these counted as nothing — we had lost Ken. It was little consolation to me that some of the others gave me credit for having shot down the German.

Ken had been very popular with the mechanics, and the next morning his fitter, Gilbert, almost tearful at the loss of '*his* pilot', asked me if there were any chance of his being allowed to qualify as a pilot or even as an observer so that he could avenge his death.

"They needn't give me any stripes, as long as they let me fight," he pleaded.

Such was the feeling of the majority of the mechanics for the fighting pilots; but Gilbert was too old, and good fitters were scarce.

Three days later Mick and I had an opportunity of taking tea at 'The Queen of Sheba's'. On entering the room I was acutely conscious of an air of depression and tension.

Mademoiselle took our order with a polite '*Oui, monsieur*', and on her departure to make the tea Mick remarked on her apparent indifference to the absence of Kennedy.

As she was laying the cakes on the table he asked her: "Don't you wonder where our — your young friend is, mademoiselle?"

She nodded. "*Certainement, monsieur le Capitaine*, but I dare not ask. It is forbidden for us to ask any questions of the English officers. — Where is the nice English boy?" She looked round anxiously as if afraid of being overheard.

She could not speak English, so Mannock answered in the only word he knew to break it gently to her.

"Il est parti," he said.

"Parti?" She was surprised and dubiously relieved. "Parti — où?"

"Not that *parti*," Mick replied. "Parti pour toujours — il est mort."

'The Queen of Sheba', holding her dainty apron up to her mouth to suppress her sobs, hurried out of the room.

Poor mademoiselle — brave French girl, I am afraid many such episodes must have been the price of her devotion to her friendly work.

Fortunately for me I went on leave the next day.

CHAPTER VIII

ON my return from leave the gap in the flight caused by Kennedy's death had been filled by a sturdy, curly headed young Irishman, McElroy.

To differentiate between the two 'Mac's' in his flight Mick called McElroy 'McIrish', and me 'McScotch', names which stuck to us until I left the Squadron. Unlike the majority of new pilots we had had, McElroy immediately fitted into the working of the flight. A new pilot was nearly always a danger to himself and to the others; if he were too cautious he was liable to be left behind to be sniped off by an astute enemy when the flight attacked; or, if he were courageous, he was just as liable to be 'downed' in his first scrap because of his ignorance of what was going on around him. In either case, his misdemeanours were likely to incur special dangers for the rest of the flight. McElroy never caused us any anxiety. His attitude towards the war was that of a terrier that has been let loose in a rat-infested barn. Both in the mess and the rugger field his sturdy scrapping was a source of great pleasure to the flight.

During my leave Mick had brought down two more German machines, a D.F.W. and an Albatros, but as these combats were of little interest he did not give me any details. One of the few scraps he did tell me about concerned another two-seater — one of those he failed to shoot down. He emptied nearly all his ammunition into it from fairly close range and saw the (presumably) dead body of the observer hanging over the side of the fuselage. He declared that he had plastered the whole of the engine and fuselage with bullets and yet the German continued to fly east, ultimately escaping.

It was fortunate for the flight that our brave-hearted Kennedy had been replaced by such a worthy successor. The Germans were becoming more numerous, and on our patrols we saw many of them, flying in flights of anything between five and twelve machines. They seldom waited for us to attack them, and even when they were in a position to attack us they very rarely did so, contenting themselves with firing short bursts from a discreet distance at the rearmost member of the flight (myself). Occasionally, becoming tired of their tactics, I let down my double Lewis gun and rounded on them, but although they could have cut me off from the rest of the flight, they very seldom accepted the challenge.

At this time, more so than at any other, we were handicapped by the lack of speed of our Nieuports compared with the German machines. The D.F.W.s, which frequently approached the lines, and the Albatros could keep out of range, a feature of aerial warfare that annoyed us and occasionally depressed Mick. Our patrols became monotonous, and as we had been ordered to report all enemy activity on the front, a typical record read something like this:

10.55 A.M. Duty, Offensive patrol, La Bassée-Scarpe.

Report. *Observed two E.A. (enemy aircraft) two-seaters approaching La Bassée low down. Dived on these but could not get within range.*

Saw eight or nine E.A. scouts over Douai, but on climbing towards them E.A. flew east.

Returning to lines, flight was attacked by E.A. formation who fired bursts at rear Nieuports from 200 to 300 yards' range. E.A. failed to attack properly.

Observed one D.F.W. in the distance low down behind Henin Lietard.

Because of this inability to come to close quarters with the enemy Mick and I had an understanding that whichever of us was free from the responsibility of leadership would remain above the flight and some distance from it, A single machine might have a chance of escaping notice. The pilot would then be in a position to involve the Germans in a mix-up, in which condition they would drop to the level of the flight. The only weakness of this piece of tactics was that the Germans were 'wary birds' and seemed to show a decided distrust of single machines.

Mick and I held several councils with Zulu and Keen on this question, and in the end we were forced to the conclusion that the only way we could get near enough to the Germans to be sure of a scrap was to go over to 'look for trouble' alone.

This was particularly disappointing for 'A' flight and, although Mick, Tud or I occasionally took Harrison or McElroy with us, with few exceptions the only flights on which we managed to obtain hand-to-hand combats were when we were alone. To relieve the monotony of uninteresting patrols Mick practised wing-tip to wing-tip formation flying and, when the patrol-time was nearing a close, he would lose height on the German side of the lines, and then contour chase back to our side, firing at any target that presented itself. It was exhilarating, descending over hostile country to shoot at cars, troops, transport or batteries. By approaching the Germans in the trenches from the rear, we escaped a great deal of the inevitable machine-gun fire. Our enjoyment of these impromptu efforts at unorthodox harassing of the Germans caused a good deal of enthusiasm amongst the men. Mick's objects in carrying out what, at first sight, appeared to be reckless escapades, were: to keep up the spirits of the whole flight, mechanics included, and 'to teach Jerry he isn't safe even behind his own lines' as he expressed it.

Under Mick's leadership we were ever conscious of his attempts to attain a high 'morale' both in the flight and the Squadron and, in fact, in everyone with whom he came into contact. We had been sent to France to 'do a job of work', and Mick never lost an opportunity of giving encouragement to artillerymen, anti-aircraft gunners or balloon observers with whom we could co-operate. He frequently borrowed a motor-cycle and side-car in order to go up and down the line visiting the Archie gunners, and the results he achieved were so satisfactory that, later, he was sent up the line' for two days to instruct the gunners on the question of the psychology of a pilot who is being shelled. Had this spirit of voluntary co-operation between the intelligent sections of the different branches been more widespread, doubtless the war would have been waged more efficiently.

My own particular amusement was ferreting out information about what was going on behind the German lines, and with this end in view I made friends with the 'photographer' in one of the reconnaissance squadrons in our wing. This officer had a large photographic map of the whole of the front behind the German lines. On it there were many details which puzzled headquarters, and as no one seemed to have thought of any means of finding out what these were other than taking more photographs I volunteered to fly at a few hundred feet over the objects. By this time, flying low on the German side of the trenches had no terrors for me, and as I had been able to give some apparently valuable information on the constructional aspect of the Hindenburg-Drocourt trenches I volunteered to photograph important sections of it from a height of fifty or a hundred feet; or, if a cinema camera were available, to take a 'close-up' of the whole line. Major Tilney rather scoffed at the idea, but he promised to pass on my suggestion. The project never materialised.

In the type of life we were forced to adopt the greatest danger lay in 'monotony' of any sort; even constant excitement became monotonous, and from it we would seek refuge in repose. Tea-parties in 'Odette's' or 'The Queen of Sheba's' helped to dispel the war weariness that crept over us at times and, in addition to these, I discovered a wonderful sanctuary of my own at the 'Aircraft Park' at Houdain. One of the irrigation canals, a fairly deep one, only five or six feet broad, passed under the trees at the edge of the 'Park', and as someone had obligingly left a diminutive punt on it I was enabled to transport my mind back to memories of the Oxford backwaters. Lying in the punt under the overhanging branches I read several books, amongst which was a popular novel that caused many heated discussions in mess: Stephen McKenna's *Sonia*. Two relics of my schooldays often accompanied me, Spinoza's *Ethics* and a small edition of *Rochfoucauld*. Whatever work we were doing, these two were always able to remind me of my 'civilian' character.

Major Tilney showed his originality by having the mess redesigned. A bay window was let into the north wall, an open fireplace of red brick was built between the ante-room and the dining-room, and the mechanics made us some comfortable chairs and a settee, these latter being covered with balloon fabric we were able to 'draw' from Brigade Stores. The fireplace was made in Tudor style, the alcove being panelled in oak with upholstered settles at the sides. When the settee was finished we discovered that the seat was too narrow and too high to be comfortable; it was therefore put into use lying on its back so that the back formed the seat and the seat the back; in which position it formed a particularly 'reposeful' piece of furniture. Another improvement was the provision of a proper bar with a service hatch into the ante-room. Drinks in the mess were 'free', in that the drink bill was shared equally by all the members of the mess; a custom which did not lead to excessive drinking, but allowed us to extend the full hospitality of the mess to any strangers who honoured us by a visit. Before the institution of this principle the advent of admiring but thirsty gunners or infantry had thrown a severe strain on the most hospitable members of the mess.

Having 'studied' with 'Charlie' in Amiens, I had been made chief cocktail-shaker, and considerable amusement was caused by my efforts at producing an original recipe. At last I found it, a most innocuous-tasting mixture of whisky-brandy-port with two drops of grenadine per glass. Visitors, honoured and otherwise, thinking that this concoction was rather weak, usually had a second, if not a third one. In this way we were able to impress our guests with our true hospitality, for after dinner while the 'Lady Killers', as we named the '40' cocktail, were having their true mellowing effect, Mick would play his most emotional rendering of 'Caprice Viennois' and 'Ave Maria', or McElroy, who had a powerful voice, would sing Irish ballads. Our mess would have done credit to any shooting-lodge; it divorced us from the war and built up the unity of the Squadron. Tilney had completed the atmosphere by hanging sporting prints on the yellow walls.

On watching Mick's expressive face as he successfully accomplished the difficult 'double-stopping' passages in Schubert's famous 'Caprice', I was amazed at the emotional splendour of his playing. Technique was required; but there was something greater than that, something no other violinist had ever conveyed to me. Mick had the soul of an idealist, one that can endure agonies of mind and body for his ideals, can kill for his beliefs. He told us all this in his playing. Perhaps my appreciation was heightened by my knowledge of his emotions, but I noticed that many of the others were equally spellbound by the tall gaunt figure standing in the half-light at the far corner of the mess. On my telling him of this he refused to play for several days and when we finally persuaded him to do so, he insisted on turning his face to the wall.

It was unfortunate for us that the piano had such an evil repute, Rook's and Kennedy's deaths had borne out the uncanny superstition and no one dared to touch it.

On other evenings when we were not so tired, or when Major Tilney considered that a change would be good for us (or for him) we would pack ourselves into a tender and, accompanied by the Squadron car, would drive to Amiens to have one of our many so-called 'binges

Under such conditions life was very easy for us, fighting or doing our best to engage the enemy during the day, yet spending our evenings in comfort and congenial surroundings.

On the 14th September Mick received further encouragement — the award of a bar to his M.C. Zulu Lloyd, Keen, Steve Godfrey and Hall wore the white and blue ribbon, but Mick was able to add the little silver rosette in the middle of the blue section of his. By this time he had ceased to be affected by his prowess, he was merely doing his 'work'. He was unassumingly confident and the brusqueness in his manner had given way to a gentleness and almost boyish ingenuousness that made him more likeable than ever. With us and with the mechanics he was more sympathetic. Even the taciturn Harrie who had seemed to bear a grudge against our more volatile Flight Commander became really one of the 'A' flight family. This may have been caused by Mick's having come to Harrie's rescue on several occasions when the latter was in grave danger of suffering for his 'bloodhound' tactics. Do what we liked, however, we could not get Harrie 'blooded', and although Mick and I took him over on many afternoons we could not lead him to a victorious battle.

As McIrish was new and could not be expected to play any great part in the actual fighting, the more 'noteworthy' work was left to Mick, Tud and myself. In one of the rare dog-fights into which we encouraged the Germans, Tud managed to send one of them down 'out of control' and, as he had no bullet holes in his own machine, Mick was greatly encouraged.

To us, an 'out of control' report meant that our shooting had been accurate; that our bullets had found the pilot or the controls; in either case the crashing of the machine and pilot was inevitable. Such reports were 'allowed' when no one actually saw the machine bursting into flames or breaking into pieces in the air. If a machine went down in a spin there was something unmistakable in the headlong dives and zooms it made as it fell staggering towards the ground: each tumble would be followed by a sudden climbing turn, on which the doomed machine would stall, to recommence its fatal dive. In the case of a machine diving after a burst of machine-gun fire, however, we could never be sure that we had registered a direct hit on a vulnerable part of the machine. The pilot, scared by our bullets, might be using the superior diving powers of his heavier machine to evade us; or the dive might have been caused by the dead or unconscious body of the pilot falling forward on to the joy-stick. In either case, spinning or diving, we rarely had the opportunity of seeing how the enemy machine hit the ground, there were usually other matters requiring attention, reloading our guns or looking out for other hostile aircraft. The large number of our pilots who escaped from scraps only to crash to the destruction of both themselves and their machines through wounds or inoperative controls showed us that it was almost impossible to estimate the damage we were doing. As Mick had said: "Flames, or a corpse on our side of the lines, are the only direct evidence, the rest is purely circumstantial."

Our anti-aircraft batteries and infantry observation posts were very helpful in confirming what happened to Germans who dived or spun from dog-fights which took place within sight of the lines, and, as the observers and gunners knew the different types of machines flown by both sides, they were able to report direct to the Squadron concerned, giving details of the types and numbers of the enemy machines.

On confirmation from the southernmost anti-aircraft battery on our sector that Tudhope's victim had been seen to go down 'absolutely out of control' the event was cause for celebration in the flight. Tud had become the craftsman, his marksmanship had been proved and his ability to avoid being hit had shown that he was capable of helping to turn the balance in War Economics in our favour. A seasoned pilot who demonstrated his ability to destroy the enemy and at the same time, by clever flying and alertness, was able to escape the enemy's bullets was worth more than four inexperienced pilots, no matter how courageous or enthusiastic the latter were. Mannock, himself, had proved this. In the beginning he had been cautious, even timorous to the extent of being mistaken for a coward, but when his assurance developed as a result of his experience and understanding of the factors involved, he emerged as the most valuable type of fighter.

At any one period there were always six or seven pilots in the Squadron who had reached this stage of development which, unfortunately, lasted only three or four months. Nerves and health could not stand the strain much longer than this and it was then that pilots were returned to Home Establishment for a 'rest'. Hall and Godfrey had been efficient as fighters since before my arrival, and in the middle of September they were sent back to England to take part in the defending of London against the Gothas. With their departure the Squadron appeared to be breaking-up. They had shared in our 'binges', had consistently and courageously increased the Squadron's list of victories, and were both such cheery and audacious warriors that we missed them both over the lines and in the mess. They had belonged to 'C' flight which was consequently weakened by the presence of two inexperienced fighters.

We lost another of our leading fighters when Crole was given command of a flight in No. 43 Squadron which was then being equipped with Sopwith Camels.

Crole's departure was a disappointment to me, but as he had seniority because of his previous service as an observer, the promotion outside our Squadron was inevitable. As 43 were still at Auchel he very frequently came to see me, bringing with him a newly acquired pet, Bruce. What Bruce was no one ever knew, but he looked like a dog of very undecided parentage. The main colour was fawn, part of him resembled a whippet while his heavy hindquarters were so unevenly balanced, one leg being over an inch longer than the other, that his walk was a mixture of gallop and shuffle. The poor dog had apparently had a hard life in the hands of his previous owners, for at the sound of a loud cheery voice he would slink underneath my bed, but Crole, Mick and I did our best to persuade him that the world was not such a cruel place for lame mongrels. Crole and Bruce were inseparable, and when Gerry went on leave I had the honour of sharing my hut with Bruce.

One afternoon, having made a rendezvous with Mick to have tea at 'The Queen of Sheba's' in Bethune, I was returning from Douai when, after passing over Henin Lietard, I observed three Albatros approaching from the south-west. They were a thousand feet above my level, and as they drew near it became perfectly obvious that their intentions towards me were not exactly chivalrous. I was then six or seven miles behind their lines, and should have been 'cold meat'.

Their first manoeuvre, however, was slightly reassuring. When about half a mile away one of them eased off to their right so as to come behind me, while the other two started to climb, waiting until all three could attack at once. Under these circumstances, I had no alternative but to let down my double Lewis gun so that it could fire upwards, and to wait for them to attack. Putting my nose down slightly to gather additional speed for a quick manoeuvre, I thought of what Mick, Tudhope and I should have done had the positions been reversed. Almost certainly only one of us would have attacked, while the other two turned back to cut off the line of retreat.

The two ahead of me dived in a half-hearted manner, letting off their guns simultaneously before they were within effective range. As the third one opened fire and all three were diving at the same time, I determined to make a fight for it — to turn east, away from the lines, and to come up underneath them before they had had time to realise what had happened to me. The two in the front, scared of coming down to my level, overshot their mark while, after making a circular turn on a vertical bank, I pulled out immediately underneath No. 3.

This was a position I liked, and while the German was turning to one side and another trying to find me, I sent a stream of tracer and armour piercer straight up into the front of the fuselage. The machine, yellow underneath, seemed to stagger, and then dived almost vertically towards the ground.

The other two, witnessing this and possibly mindful of their orders to attack only when sure of success, decided that a further attempt was not justified. They headed north-east, the second one straggling far behind the first. I saw this in a second and, fearing that I had not 'done in' No. 3 completely, dived helter-skelter after him in the direction of our lines. He crashed straight into a field to the southeast of Lens. I descended almost to the ground and contour-chased over the trenches to Mazingarbe.

Mannock almost exploded when I told him. "What! — why the Hake wasn't I there too? — just my Pygmalion luck!" He wanted to go straight up again, but I persuaded him that cream cakes in 'The Queen of Sheba's' were indicated as a celebration. "We can have dinner in Bethune to-night if you get yours later on," I declared.

On telephoning my report to the Squadron, Major Tilney told me that Barlow had been killed. Poor Barlow, we had had many friendly scragging matches in the mess, and because of the sporting and manly attitude he had always shown, his death came as a great shock to me — and to the whole Squadron.

During tea Mick paused in the middle of an argument on the rival merits of French and British diplomacy. "Look here, young Mac, that one this afternoon pulls you level with me this month. I can't darned well have that — have to look to my laurels."

In my mind there was no question of any competition with Mick. This propensity of his for establishing friendly rivalries, unspoilt by any tinge of jealousy, always amused me. When he could manage it he would even play Tudhope and myself against each other, purely with the object of 'livening things up' and of getting the best out of both of us. Mick has won the title of 'King of Air Fighters', the name given to the book by Squadron Leader Ira Jones, D.S.O., M.C., D.F.C., M.M., but after his first excusable excitement no one had less desire to be considered as the leader, the commanding officer, or the 'King' than Mick. His only objective was victory for the Flight, the Squadron and the Army.

Before we left the ground at Mazingarbe, he declared that the damage wrought by the flight was going to be increased still further 'even though it's got to be a balloon'.

True enough, he succeeded in cutting another notch in our totem pole by sending one of the enemy down to destruction in the lines just east of Offy. I never heard the details, for unless there was something particularly interesting about them we never discussed our scraps.

Barlow had come down on our side of the lines, and when his body was brought back to the Squadron I wanted to see him again to pay my last respects, but Major Tilney advised me not to. "It would make too much impression on you, he's terribly smashed up," he said.

The next day we held one of our flight 'Discussion Meetings', at which Mick insisted on the necessity of pressing for victories. I remember his saying at the end, "We'll teach them they can't darned well show their noses near the line."

Almost as if in defiance of this dictum, one particularly daring Albatros pilot succeeded in carrying out three or four successful raids on our side of the lines. We heard several reports, all of which credited him with having destroyed several of our balloons and with having shot down three or four R.E.Ss and one A.W.

Mannock was furious, and for two days he, Tud or I patrolled frantically over the lines waiting to catch the German on his next venture. There was one feature about war flying on which most fighters agree: once a pilot has been bitten by the balloon-strafing-bug he cannot resist further temptation. We

131

knew by this fellow's successes that he would come over again, and we hoped to be there when he did.

On the evening of the 26th September he shot down a balloon, and in the early morning of the 27th another was sent to its flaming end, along with another R.E.8. In the afternoon all three of us were at Mazingarbe, two waiting while the other patrolled. There was no sign of the German. At last Mick had a brain-wave, one of those inspirations that arise after some careful thinking.

"That fellow won't come over this afternoon. He's going to come over this evening when we are at dinner — but we aren't going to have dinner until after we've got him. We'll sit here till dark."

Mick then telephoned one of the K.B. sections to ascertain if his suppositions were correct. Every one of the raids had been carried out at the orthodox British mealtimes during which our activity usually slackened. Lone flyers were not likely to be in the air, and the official patrols took place at too great a height to be a danger to a low-flying machine. The German was clever.

We held a debate on the tactics we should employ were we in the position of the German, and I ended the argument by saying that if I attempted to emulate the raider, and knew of the existence of a hostile landing-ground so close to the trenches, I should have one of the forward observation posts keeping a close look out for machines descending in the vicinity.

"That clinches it then," Mick said, "we've got to let them see us returning to Bruay, no humbug about it. Then we can come back when it's nearly dark and patrol above the balloons."

He telephoned to the K.B. sections asking them if they would send the balloons up *without any observers in the baskets*. In the economics of war a balloon without an observer is 'cheap' bait for an enemy of the Albatros pilot's calibre.

After a refresher in the mess we returned to the aerodrome, arranging that Tud was to patrol behind the two balloons nearest the Scarpe, Mick was to take those between Souchez and Mazingarbe, and I was to guard the two between the landing-ground and the La Bassée Canal.

The sun had gone down, and as I patrolled solemnly over the two balloons I began to wonder whether Mannock had not been wrong, for soon it would be too dark to see the balloons. In the dim haze I searched for the sight of a camouflaged attacker. While patrolling, a feeling of nausea gradually stole over me and my head began to ache; a throbbing sickening feeling. As darkness descended my discomfort increased and I was about to return to Bruay when one of the southern balloons went up in flames.

A balloon on fire is a nasty sight. First a small burst of flame which is soon followed by a huge column of fire as the inflammable gas is liberated. The balloon drops slowly at first and then begins to disintegrate, pieces of the burning fabric whirling about and falling slowly through the air. I did not wait for the end, but flew straight for the next balloon in the line, the one south of Petit Sains. It was almost too dark to see an enemy machine, so I circled frantically round the balloon for ten minutes before my throbbing head and sickness made me fly back to Bruay.

I struggled out of the machine, and the mechanics helped me to take off my cap and coat. I was leaning against the corner strut of the hangar when Major Tilney ran up.

"Come on, Mac, Tud's got him down, jump into the car and come with us."

Despite my feelings I was overjoyed and climbed into the Squadron car beside the C.O. and Wolff, a new pilot. Tudhope was in front.

When we were outside the town on the Lens road Tilney turned to me, saying: "Good Heavens, you're shivering- — you had better take my coat, I've got a Burberry here!"

I was grateful for the warmth of his fur-lined coat and told him that I felt 'rotten'.

"Never mind, Mac — you'll feel better when you see the lovely one Tud has brought down. It's near Souchez."

We had to drive up to Bully-Grenay before we could get on to the Souchez road, and as the roads were pocked with shell holes the driver switched on his lights — but not for long, as a stentorian-voiced sentry yelled: "Put those bloody lights out."

We had to crawl along the road till we reached the Souchez cross-roads. There, on a mound of bricks from the demolished houses, was the German machine — a beautiful Albatros, with a plywood fuselage. Several Canadians had gathered round it, while Mannock had mounted guard, defiantly holding the inquisitive back at the point of a Very pistol.

His greeting to Tudhope was typical. "Here the Conquering Hero comes," he yelled, and dashed forward to congratulate him.

The crashed machine was a sorry sight. We examined it for some time until the captain commanding the Kite Balloon section invited us into their mess to have a drink. We then learnt that there had been an observer in the balloon and that the German had fired at him as he descended on his parachute. The Canadian infantry had wanted to 'say a few words about it', but Mannock had restrained them with his Very pistol.

Tudhope was excited, but as Mannock was still more so, the remainder of the K.B. section were under the impression that the latter had brought down the German. My headache was still bad, and as I quietly drank a whisky to my surprise everyone said 'Sir' when addressing me.

When I asked one of them the reason for this he pointed to my coat where, truly enough, there was a crown on the shoulder-strap. I then remembered it was Major Tilney's coat. We explained the reason for the confusion there had been about the 'victor' and the 'Major' and, as the occasion demanded it, more drinks were placed before us. My headache persisted, and it was a relief to me when we again climbed into the car for the return journey.

I did not learn the cause of my indisposition till the next morning when Sergeant Smart told me that my propeller boss had been almost burnt through by some of the bolts having come loose. An examination revealed the fact that there was considerable play on the propeller, which had resulted in the whole of the vibration of the engine being transmitted to the machine. In the air, as long as the engine was firing correctly, one could not have noticed such a defect.

It was a wet morning, and as there could not be any flying anyway my 'Silver Queen' was 'laid up' to get a new engine.

That was the first free day we had had since my return from leave, and it was with considerable enjoyment Mannock, Tudhope and I debated as to how we should spend it.

"Come on — I've got it. Let's have our photographs taken properly, we three. We may never have another chance."

Deciding that Houdain, being the Army Headquarters, was sure to have a professional photographer, we walked into the village to ascertain. Enquiries revealed that there was one photographer, an invalid, who earned sufficient to maintain a small studio, and in defiance of superstition we had our photographs taken together.

On the way from the aerodrome I remembered Mannock's remark concerning his 'eye', and, on asking him the reason for it he told us part of his history.

At the beginning of the war he was employed on the telephone service in Turkey and had been interned when the Turks joined forces with the Germans. After a year of imprisonment the Turks decided that on account of his defective eyesight he would be of little use to the fighting forces, and they repatriated him as a 'crock'.

He laughed heartily at the recollection and said: "If they had known that I was destined to do so much damage to their beloved Hun Allies they would have put a price on my head instead of sending me home."

On my asking him how he had managed to pass the medical tests, he told us that as he knew he could never pass the eyesight test he took care to be at the examination-rooms before the doctor arrived. He nearly failed in his object, for the doctor appeared a few minutes later, before he had had time to memorise the forty letters and numerals on the board.

Because of this he would have had little chance of succeeding had the doctor chosen the wrong eye first.

"And just think — the old josser covered my bad eye first and gave me time to make sure of the letters before he covered the good one. Had he done it the other way round I should now be a civilian looking with envy at you blighters in your uniforms."

He swore us to secrecy as he was still afraid that his eye would invalidate his commission.

Walking down the hill into Houdain in the drizzle I learnt the details of Tud's success the previous evening.

Mannock, with a dud engine, had landed at Mazingarbe, and while having a cigarette and keeping a watchful eye on the front had seen Tudhope landing. Tud's engine was missing badly, and as Mannock walked out to meet him the southern balloon caught fire.

"Look, Tud — go on, you'll get the blighter," he yelled.

Tudhope had taken off across wind with violent splutters from his defective engine. After that it was only a matter of two minutes before he had shot down the German.

Mannock, with his arms linked in ours — showing his paternal feeling towards us — said that Tud's victory pleased him more than if he himself had brought the German to the ground.

This friendship that existed between fighting pilots was an enlightenment to me. Scrapping alongside each other, sharing the same hopes and fears and with the same mutual respect each for the others, brought fellows much closer than would be possible in civilian life. Our lives were at stake, and it is only when the most powerful instinct, of self-preservation, takes command that one can form a true estimate of the character of one's friends. Our sense of character values became more acute.

We welcomed the rain. We were tired of flying, and Major Tilney's letter to his mother aptly describes the condition of the whole Squadron. He said:

Thank goodness the weather has broken. I hope it will be dud for a bit. My fellows are dead beat. Six weeks' solid flying.

This was quite true. In August and September we had been scrapping almost every day and both desperate fights and 'victories' had become so much part of our lives that events became no longer worthy of record. So great had been the enthusiasm of the whole squadron that I doubt if more than a third of the time spent over the lines was taken up with official patrols.

Steve Godfrey, Hall, Zulu Lloyd and Crole had all done well, while Keen, the quietest of all of us, had excelled himself.

In the afternoon Mannock, Tudhope, McElroy and I went into Doullens and later in the day drove on to Amiens, where we had one of our private 'Flight Celebrations'. Tudhope was by nature the most stolid of the party, and my admiration for him was increased when I saw that his spectacular conquest had had no more effect on him than had the bullet hole in his collar on the memorable day when his strut was burnt.

During the month there were two disastrous crashes: one, in which Nutter, a new pilot, was killed after diving straight into the ground at the corner of the aerodrome, and the other, in which the indomitable P. W. Smith was involved. P. W. had never completely succeeded in overcoming the Nieuport's propensity for spinning, and it was no uncommon sight to see his machine performing its crazy corkscrew descent towards the ground. Every time it happened we had thought that it must be the last time — but to our amazement P. W. continued to arrive safely at Bruay. In September, however, his Nieuport proved more stubborn than ever, and in full view of the spectators at a special 'Army Show' at Houdain it spun from ten thousand feet, straight into the ground.

P. W., when they reverently disentangled him from the wreckage, had almost every bone in his body broken, one eye was missing, and one of his thumbs had been torn off by the firing lever on the joy-stick. He was unconscious, and when we enquired for him the next day we found that he was still alive, but unconscious.

Our enquiries for six weeks resulted in the same reply. Then P. W. recovered consciousness.

He was flying a year after this.

*

In connection with this victory of Tudhope's an amusing coincidence occurred ten years afterwards.

Several peace-time acquaintances had forgathered in an hotel lounge and were relating war stories. I had recounted the events that led up to the destroying of Tudhope's victim without giving the date or names when, to my surprise, one of the others offered to complete the story.

"That happened at the end of September 1917, and it was Mannock, the V.C., who brought it down at Souchez. I was there," he said.

I corrected him about Mannock, and asked him where he was at the time.

lie laughed uproariously. "I was the observer in the balloon just south of your landing-ground. When the other one went down in flames, the fellows on the ground telephoned me to 'Jump', but as I had never done a 'drop' before I was sitting on the edge of the basket trying to pluck up courage to let go, when I heard your machine. I thought it was the Hun and was scared stiff till I saw your circles. My relief was so great that I fell over backwards into the basket and stayed there until they hauled the balloon down."

CHAPTER IX

THE rain that fell on the day following Tudhope's victory at Souchez heralded a long spell of broken weather, of wet drizzly days and heavy showers punctuated by periods of clear cold weather. We regarded this as an unwelcome deterrent to our progress, the resultant inactivity being too great a change after two months of almost continuous flying. Our only consolation was that the Germans were not doing any 'work', they seemed to be more reluctant to take to the air in bad weather, and on the few patrols we managed to carry out we rarely encountered a German.

To make it possible for the flight to stalk any enemy pilot who did venture out, Mick got into the habit of climbing to fourteen or fifteen thousand feet on our side of the lines so that we could cross into enemy territory to the south of the Scarpe or even on the Bapaume front. After crossing the lines he climbed steadily towards Douai where we turned north-west so that we could command a view of the whole of our sector and at the same time be hidden in the sun's rays, particularly blinding during those clear hours.

I noticed that Mick was taking us rather high, right round the full scale of my aneroid, a twenty-thousand-feet instrument, but as there was nothing to report on several of such flights no one made any remark. Flying at that height I felt a bitter, bone-stiffening cold, but as none of the others said anything I thought that my circulation must be at fault. One day, when my aneroid was on the twenty-thousand line (its limit) Mick's machine began to spin, only two turns, before he pulled straight again. In the rarefied atmosphere the planes have not the same grip on the air, and on making any sudden movement the machine drops and — in the case of a Nieuport — spins.

"Did you see that?" Mick said when we landed. "My machine's as bad as poor Peter Wylie's. It surely couldn't have been a shell at fifteen thousand feet."

"What!" Tudhope and Harrison expostulated. "Twenty-two thousand."

It took a good deal of persuasion to convince him that we had been 'on the ceiling', the uppermost flying limit of our Nieuports. Mick's aneroid had stuck at fifteen thousand, but he insisted that in the future the patrols should be made as high as possible. Flying at a height of over four miles, our field of vision allowed us to watch the whole of the area between Ypres and Douai and, so that he would not fail to observe everything that took place on the Front, Mick set out to buy a pair of binoculars from the Ordnance Depot.

As usual he brought out the amusing side of the occasion by demanding a *telescope*.

"This isn't a naval stores," the man behind the counter told him, "we only have prismatic binoculars."

"What did I tell you — I want a telescope; what's the use of having two eye-pieces when you can only use one. However, I must have them."

On Tud's asking him why on earth he wanted them, Mick replied, pointing at me:

"I can't have that fellow beating me at anything to do with fighting. He's not going to see anything I can't."

There was a good deal of friendly rivalry among the three of us, but on the question of 'vision' I had always scored over Mick's one good eye.

As the weather grew colder our mess became more and more popular with the Canadians, the Archie gunners, and friends in other squadrons. One Canadian, a newcomer to the mess, asked to meet the pilot who had brought down the two-seater on our side of the lines. On being introduced to Mick he dived his hand into his tunic pocket and produced a neat wristlet-watch.

"Now — you needn't take this unless you want to, and you had better not, until I tell you all about it," he said to Mick.

Mannock examined the watch and looked enquiringly at the Canadian. The latter then told him that the watch had been taken from the dead German and that seven or eight successive 'winners' of the watch had been killed. Someone had given voice to the suspicion that there was a 'hoodoo' over it, and as no one in the company would wear it, the men had asked their company commander to deliver it to the officer that had killed the German pilot.

Mannock strapped the evil talisman on his arm, and after thanking the Canadian asked him to have a drink.

"Thanks very much — I will; but to get this business finished properly you'd better give me a receipt to show to the fellows."

Finding that he was welcomed by the Squadron the Canadian asked if he might bring some of his friends, and while they were out of the line on 'rest' several of them visited us.

They were apparently unwilling to accept our hospitality without giving something in return, and before they went back to the trenches most of our pilots had souvenirs: bayonets, rifles, Mausers and even bombs. We did not know that these latter had not been unloaded until one of the pilots was attempting to get the top off a rifle grenade with a screw-driver.

"Hey," the Canadian called out, "you've got to treat those things with respect, there's a detonator inside that fellow."

This remark caused consternation amongst the possessors of 'bomb' souvenirs, and as I was the only member of the Squadron that knew anything about German grenades it fell to my lot to unload them.

Mannock had a good deal of fun out of this, and pretended to make wide detours to avoid passing my hut.

One evening I was sitting inside wondering if I dared attempt to take a rusted percussion grenade to pieces, while Mannock was standing at the door watching me and questioning me about the German bombs.

"If this one is properly loaded it's got no fewer than seven detonators in it," I had told him, when there was the sound of footsteps.

Mannock looked round.

"Here — you. You'd better walk round that way. Mac's taking a bomb to pieces, one of the kind that doesn't 'fizz' first."

It was a clever adaptation of the 'Bairnsfather' cartoon in which Alf says to Bert who is sitting on a twelve-inch shell attempting to knock the fuse-cap off with a hammer and chisel: "Give it a good 'ard 'un, Bert: you can generally 'ear 'em fizzing a bit first if they are a-going to explode."

Major Tilney was in his hut and, coming over to see how much was joke and how much truth, told me that I had no right to undertake such dangerous work.

We had many jolly evenings in the mess but, being confined to the ante-room all day, if it were wet, we welcomed the trips to Amiens.

One evening about a dozen of us were dining in the Beaufort Hotel, in a private room on the first floor, when an incident occurred which gave Mick a good chance of displaying his tact. General Shephard was with us, and as the meal progressed the evening was livened by a battle royal in which we used as missiles anything that came to our hands, crumbs, sugar and portions of lobster shell that remained on our plates. Zulu, Tud, McElroy, Pettigrew, Wolff, Wallwork, Gollop, Warden and Rusden all joined in the fray, and the battle proceeded merrily until someone accidentally threw a lobster claw through the open window that overlooked the street.

I looked out to see if anyone had been hit, and caught a glimpse of an officer, a major, trying to pull the sharp end of the claw from his head. I told the others to expect a row, and there was a sudden silence as we heard loud voices outside on the stairs.

Mannock held up his hand. "Leave it to me, and remember, *we don't know what happened.*"

The door was thrown open and the irate major stood there. He was holding his forage-cap in one hand, while the other, covered with blood, was massaging his bald head.

"Good heavens — what's wrong, Sir," Mannock jumped up, "can I help you?"

"Wrong be damned — which of you swine threw that thing at me?" He threatened us with arrest, and it was several minutes before Mick succeeded in stemming his torrent of abuse.

"I'm sure no one here would throw anything at you, Sir — if he did he'd be up before the orderly-room to-morrow. If that claw came from here it was entirely an accident. Sit down and have a drink — but first let me introduce you to — *General Shephard.*" Conscious that he had not behaved with the dignity and decorum demanded from an officer of field rank, the stranger was so taken aback by the presence of our Brigadier that he subsided into a chair and willingly accepted the wine Mick poured out for him. We then apologised to him for the accident, and Mick attended to the cut on his head.

Despite the high spirits, our so-called 'binges' usually passed off quietly, the principal excitement coming on the way home. As it was always late before we departed and A.P.M.s were not so much in evidence, Tilney and I frequently had races between the Squadron car and the tender, he driving the former while I took the latter. One night, driving with Zulu and Tudhope beside me, we were singing the popular South African song:

Vat jou goed en trek Ferreira
Daar le die ding,
Daar le die ding

when there were bellicose yells from the inside of the tender. In my enthusiasm for learning the refrain I had been keeping time by swinging the car from side to side of the road, with dire results on those sitting on the two uncomfortable inside seats. Two choruses had proved sufficient to throw them into a heap in the middle of the tender.

There were threats of all sorts of vengeance, but when we ultimately arrived at Bruay everyone was so cold and miserable that, instead of murdering me as they had promised, they had to express their gratitude for an egg nogg I had prepared for them in the bar.

In the morning I found a dainty pair of women's undergarments in my coat pocket, put there by some miscreant of the previous evening. This was the second pair that had come into my possession through no volition on my part and I decided to get rid of one of them. Mick seemed the most likely subject for a jape and, remembering that he had used a pair of silk stockings instead of streamers on his struts, I decided that his third streamer should appropriately be replaced by the 'undies'.

When he saw them he held a conference with us as to whether he would be liable for court-martial for decorating one of His Majesty's aeroplanes in this way and, to find out if the 'undies' would be visible from the ground, he did a tour round the aerodrome at two thousand feet — the lingerie ballooning out realistically.

"What did it look like?" he asked on landing.

Sergeant Smart stifled the prospect of our 'following' a pair of 'ladies' panties into battle, by saying: "It looked exactly as if you had hung the washing out on your machine, Sir."

On one of our trips I found a bedraggled kitten mewing for help in the middle of the road on which the rain was beating down in torrents. Filled with sympathy because of its shivering misery, I put it in the pocket of my warm, sheepskin-lined coat and took it back to the camp. On taking it out I saw that it had dried into a fluffy ball with beautiful grey and black markings.

After enquiring where I had found it Mick held it aloft for everyone to see.

"By Jove, we've got a fine cat now — anyone got a name for it? Anyone got a name for a cat?"

Several orthodox names were suggested, and it appeared as if 'Sonia' were going to win, when the kitten (fortunately for me) took the opportunity of doing what all cats and dogs have to do on occasions.

"Look out, Mick!" someone called.

Mick placed the kitten gingerly on the floor and wrathfully shook his finger at it while it mewed up at him.

"That's what we're going to call you — Piddle."

This name stuck and everyone forgot the origin until, a little later we were entertaining the matron and some of the nurses from a neighbouring hospital.

We were having tea in the ante-room when our pet came in at the door and stalked majestically across towards the dining-room.

"What a lovely cat!" the Matron observed. "Puss-puss."

Our orphan paid no attention.

"What do you call it?" Matron asked.

Major Tilney blushed, some of the others sniggered, but Mick, with his usual resourcefulness, called, "Fiddle, Fiddle."

But Piddle did not deign to respond to any such name and, as she disappeared through the door, Mick dashed after her. "Come here, you nameless huzzy."

In the early part of October the G.O.C. carried out a much-needed improvement in our equipment. The poor old Nieuports had been outclassed by the Albatros so long, and so many of our patrols had ended in the frustration of our hopes of getting to close quarters with the enemy, that the Squadron was gradually equipped with a much faster machine, the S.E.5a. These were capable of attaining a speed of 120 m.p.h. on the level, their diving speed was over 200 m.p.h. against the Nieuports' 150 and, in addition, they were equipped with a Vickers gun synchronised to fire through the propeller as well as the standard Lewis gun mounted on the top plane.

At first we were optimistic about our prospects of fighting on S.E.s. The German Albatros or Halberstadts would no longer be able to evade us. No. 56 Squadron had already shown what magnificent work could be done on a fast machine: but before a fortnight had elapsed we had learnt the limitations of the S.E.5s that had been supplied to us.

The particular engines with which they were fitted were so unreliable that within a fortnight our pilots had over twenty forced landings through engine failure, my own record for one week being four.

For nearly three weeks we experimented with the S.E.5s, machine-gun practice, formation flying, and stunting, with only occasional patrols, nearly all of which were split up because of engine failures. This had a particularly demoralising effect on the whole Squadron, and for those three weeks we did not place a single enemy machine to our credit.

Being forced to land on the German side only to be peacefully taken prisoner through the inherent weakness of our engines appeared to us as an ignominious ending to a fighting career. Mannock was furious and, as I had had to give up my beloved 'Silver Queen' for a machine that consistently let me down, my attitude towards the S.E.5s was not exactly friendly.

Owing to the apparent inactivity of the Squadron, General Trenchard paid us another visit to ascertain the cause of the trouble, for until the advent of the S.E.s the Squadron's record had been a particularly good one. General Trenchard favoured the machines which had been demonstrated by '56' to be the best on either side of the Front, and he was disappointed that in '40' they had so far proved to be less efficient than the Nieuports. Added to the engine trouble was the disconcerting fact that the Vickers guns were prone to jam and, owing to bad fitting of the Constantinesco gearing for synchronising the gun to the propeller, many of our propellers were damaged.

While General Trenchard was standing on the aerodrome discussing the machines with Major Tilney, Mick landed. The General's A.D.C. was talking to me, and as Mannock taxied in furiously the A.D.C. asked: "Who is that?" and on being informed, he added: "Well, let's hear what *he* has to say!"

Mick was in a temper and, without giving me time to say who the visitor was, he burst out: "Look at this Vickers gun — look at it — fired two rounds — pop-pop — and then stopped, jammed properly. If I had had my good old Nieuport I could have had two nice juicy Huns."

He pressed the firing lever again to show us that the gun would not fire, and then climbed out of the cockpit.

"What do you think of the machines though," the A.D.C. asked.

"Pretty awful with these engines and guns. The machines themselves are all right I suppose — but give me a Nieuport any day," Mick replied.

As we were walking round to the mess I could hear the C.O. talking to Mannock just behind us, and the latter replying loudly: "I'm sorry, Sir, but if it results in my getting my good old Nieuport back, I don't care."

Afterwards when I tackled him on the gun question he had to admit that as the Vickers was additional to the Lewis, he had been at no real disadvantage.

"Yes — but what is the use of carrying a gun that is no use to you. When it does fire it goes pop-pop-pop, as slowly as one of Jerry's guns, and if the mechanism isn't right you shoot your 'prop'. These are all things that need consideration by the authorities, and if *we* don't say things outright, nothing will be done about it."

His outburst before the G.O.C. had the anticipated result, for one miserable afternoon a day or two later, when we were confined to the ante-room because of the rain, a stranger entered and stood at the door looking at us gathered round our cosy fireplace. He had taken off his hat, and as he was wearing a trench-coat we could not ascertain his rank until Mannock called out:

"Good afternoon to you, stranger. Take off your coat and come into the warmth," and in preparation for offering the hospitality of the mess, "Orderly."

As the visitor discarded his coat I could see Mick fixing his eye on the blue tabs of a staff officer.

"And may I ask who you are?" Mannock demanded slightly less cordially — he hated 'tabs' of any description, but blue ones in particular.

"I'm gunnery officer at Headquarters," the stranger replied. "I've come over —"

Mannock allowed him no time to finish.

"You've got something to do with Vickers guns then? — and you dare to come into this mess!" Without pausing to hear the reply he called out at the top of his voice: "Orderly — Orderly — quick!"

Simmonds appeared at the mess doorway.

"Yes, Sir?"

"Fetch a hatchet," Mick ordered.

"A-a-a hatchet, Sir — what for?" was all Simmonds could stammer.

Mannock spelt it out. "H-A-T-C-H-E-T, now do you understand. I want a hatchet."

Simmonds was about to turn away to carry out this unusual request when Mannock grinned. Turning to the stranger he said: "Now you know my sentiments — what'll you have to drink?"

It turned out that General Trenchard had sent his gunnery expert post-haste to us to give us some instruction in the working of the synchronising gear.

Shortly afterwards a gunnery officer, Douglas, was posted to the Squadron, and our Vickers guns ceased to trouble us. As the Vickers fired through the propeller and the Lewis was mounted on the top plane above the level of the propeller, the tracks of the bullets would normally have been parallel, but it was left to our discretion as to how we were to use them, whether to make the trajectories meet at fifty or a hundred yards. The sound of the two different guns was a source of amusement to me, the hurried clacky-clack of the Lewis and the slow, deliberate pop-pop of the Vickers. After the delightful 'music' of my double Lewis even the combination of Vickers and Lewis sounded tame. Because of the scarcity of Lewis guns an application to have my double Lewis returned proved abortive, the infantry needed them more than we did. The mounting for the single gun, however, was an improvement on Steve Godfrey's and mine, the bracket was clamped to a toothed and curved brass support in such a way that we could fix the gun at any desired angle, but in such a position we had to guide the machine instead of being able to traverse the gun as I had done with my own mounting.

Many of the new pilots who had not flown Nieuports during the summer, or who disliked the 'silver hawks', were more enthusiastic about the S.E.5s. Being new and having been accustomed to the habitual forced landings at instructional schools, they did not appreciate the grave dangers of a weak engine; nor had they the comparison to make between the quickness of control of the Nieuport and the heavy sluggishness of the S.E.5. They had therefore much more confidence in the new machines than we had.

Two outstanding examples of these junior pilots were McElroy and Wolff. Although both had proved to be able pilots on Nieuports, it was only when they were given S.E.5S that their full capabilities were demonstrated. McElroy had always said that he never felt comfortable in a Nieuport, but in the S.E. he snuggled into the cosy cockpit and became a 'warrior'. Wolff was only about five feet two or three, and as the Lewis gun on the S.E. was out of his reach a special seat had to be made to raise him high enough to grip the handle of the gun. Report had it that, on attempting to enlist wearing his school cap, the recruiting officer had told Wolff to go away and to return with headgear more becoming to a fighter. With the few shillings remaining from his pocket money the 'schoolboy' succeeded in buying a bowler, many sizes too big for him, and with this pulled well down over his head he had been accepted. Anyway, he found himself in '40' at the tender age of eighteen.

One morning at the end of October I had the unpleasant duty of taking Keen's flight over the lines. I did not know the capabilities of any of the pilots as they were nearly all new, and 'A' flight had kept very much to itself. Before leaving the ground, noticing the extreme youth of the junior member, Wolff, I told him to fly as close to me as possible, and, if we got into a scrap, to 'stick to me like grim death'.

Apart from the fact that I was leading an untried flight, the idiosyncrasies of our engines would not have warranted a really offensive patrol, and I contented myself with flying northwards and southwards between La Bassée and the Scarpe and only two or three miles on the German side of the line. Archie attacked us half-heartedly, and after an hour it appeared as if the patrol were going to finish as most of our other S.E.5 patrols had done, without anything worth recording, when my suspicions were directed to another machine.

This was a heavy two-seater, so closely resembling a D.H.4 as to deceive the whole flight. We had twice passed within a quarter of a mile of it before I began to wonder why a bombing machine was flying up and down over the lines without being Archied. On the next turn southwards from La Bassée I determined to investigate, and as we approached the two-seater I manoeuvred so that we should pass within two hundred yards of it and three or four hundred feet above. While carrying this out I espied several machines approaching from the south-east about two thousand feet above our level.

They were some distance away, and as the two-seater on close inspection turned out to have iron crosses on the planes I hurriedly 'wagged' my wings and fired a burst into the cockpits at point-blank range. The proximity of the Albatros precluded any possibility of watching what ultimately happened to it, as I had to turn round in an attempt to avoid an attack by the enemy scouts and at the same time to retreat without obviously fleeing from them.

When I saw that the German pilots were determined to come to grips, I wagged my wings savagely and signed to Wolff and Bion, flying on my right and left respectively, to let their Lewis guns down. As soon as this was done, I wheeled about quickly to come face to face with the Albatros that were already diving on us.

My tactics evidently threw them into confusion, for the leader pulled up, allowing me to give him a short burst, but in a few seconds the others had rallied and attacked us with vigour. Having new pilots with me I could not afford to risk attacking any individual machines, but had to 'stunt' for all I was worth to keep the Germans on the alert, firing both guns whenever an Albatros was within the possible traverse of the 'spray' of tracer.

After a minute or so of this the Germans tired of the combat and dived off eastwards.

Throughout the fight young Wolff had almost literally 'stuck to me', and even on the worst turns and twists I had been reassured to see him following only fifteen or twenty feet distant from my wing-tip. Greatly to my relief, too, the others fell in behind my machine, and when the patrol-time expired we returned to the aerodrome intact, or almost so.

In case of accidents I had made a practice when leading 'A' flight of allowing the flight to land first, and on this occasion I was disappointed to see two of the machines crashing in the middle of the aerodrome. When my own turn came, as soon as the machine touched the ground the undercarriage buckled up and the machine turned over. I had forgotten the possibility of a tyre being punctured by bullets.

Only when we were filling in our combat reports was the true heinousness of my crime in allowing a German flight to attack me from above made apparent. I heard Bion and the others discussing the scrap and Wolff asking in a surprised tone: "What scrap? I saw only the two-seater. I thought Mac was stunting."

Wolff had not seen any of the seven Albatros that had attacked us. He had thought that the stunting was a sign of jubilation on my part, but when the flight sergeant came into the orderly-room to tell us that Wolff's machine had over fifty bullet holes in it, eight of these being within a foot of where his head had been, the 'schoolboy' had definite evidence that he had been in a real scrap.

Needless to say I received a good deal of criticism for not avoiding a fight when I had new pilots with me, and was sitting in the orderly-room feeling rather despondent when Mick came in.

"So you did land that mob into some Huns then — do 'em all good."

I had to admit that the two-seater had obviously been a decoy.

"What!" he almost yelled. "Of all the bloody cheek — the Hun putting out a decoy for *you*, after we've been doing our damnedest to get them to attack us. I don't believe it."

It struck me as being rather ironical, particularly as our anti-aircraft gunners confirmed an 'out of control' for me. If it were a trap it was an exceedingly foolish one, for had I had Tud, McElroy and Harrison with me, the Albatros also might have paid a heavier price for their temerity. On many occasions Mick, Tud, Harrie and I had intentionally allowed the enemy to get above us hoping that by so doing we could persuade them to attack.

The feature of the scrap which impressed me most, however, was the brilliant flying of the young pilot and the cheery grin he wore when he was shown the bullet holes in his machine —

yet, with such obvious flying ability he had not even seen the German that had so nearly ended his life.

After my machine was repaired, headquarters decided that I was to become the experimental pilot of the Squadron, and to this end my machine was fitted with an *automatic* oxygen apparatus and a special bomb carrier. The oxygen made me so sick on my first attempt to use it that I discarded it with a recommendation that the supply should be under the control of the pilot. The bomb carrier, on the other hand, was more acceptable, and both Tudhope and I practised bomb-dropping on the aerodrome. The carrier accommodated four 20-pound Cooper bombs, and as the performance of the machine did not seem to be impaired, I looked forward to being provided with live bombs instead of the dummies with which we had to practise.

This venture opened up a new field of activity for me, and when the bombs arrived I had already made up my mind as to my first two objectives: the two star anti-aircraft batteries.

Unfortunately for me I reckoned without my engine. In practice we dropped the bombs from one thousand feet. Now, to make reasonably sure of hitting my real target with the live bombs I decided to descend to five or six hundred feet. All went well until just after I had dropped all four bombs and was climbing towards the lines. Then my engine spluttered, coughed and finally stopped.

This happened at about one thousand feet, nearly a mile on the German side of the lines, and had the wind not been behind me I should have had no chance of getting back. I kept up a fair speed in the glide, and passing over the German trenches the silence of my engine allowed me to hear the full nastiness of the machine-guns that were firing at me. I could not waste height in dodging the fire, so I simply waited either to be hit or to see the uniforms in the trenches change from grey to khaki.

I succeeded in coming down between our front line and the support trenches just behind a mound which partially screened me from the German trenches. There was not a space of even ten yards on which to land, and as a crash seemed inevitable I held the machine off the ground as long as possible. She pancaked gently with her undercarriage in a shell-hole and her lower planes flat on the ground. Not even the propeller was broken.

The Canadians, anticipating a crash, jumped out of the trenches and were making their way towards me before the machine actually touched the ground.

I climbed out hurriedly, and one of the Canadians said: "Better get down, they can reach us here."

He was evidently mistaken, for the machine-guns stopped, and we gathered round the machine to take all the removable apparatus from her as quickly as possible.

Within half an hour we were forced to cease as the German artillery began shelling the place. After a short but intense 'strafing' I was surprised to see that the machine was still intact. During the bombardment I had had time to send a telegram to the Squadron telling the C.O. where I was and asking if a tender could be sent as near as possible to collect the apparatus.

The Canadians became very enthusiastic about salving the machine and, as one of them declared that until the Jerry gunners were satisfied that they had destroyed it they would continue to send over shells in its direction, it was considered advisable either to blow it up or to move it. Eight or nine lusty Canadians managed to lift it bodily from the shell hole, and amidst much cursing carried the machine down the slope to the edge of a cutting overhanging a broken track that had once been a road.

Darkness fell, and I retired to the trench with several Canadian officers who asked me into their dug-out to have something to eat. I had been out all day and had had no food, and the pork and beans, washed down with 'Pepper' whisky, proved very acceptable. While sitting talking afterwards I was pleased to see the cheery face of Sergeant Smart looking in at me.

He explained that as they had considered it almost impossible to salve a machine from a position so close to the enemy, he had come up the line on a motorcycle to investigate the advisability of attempting it.

When he saw where the machine was he was confident that it could be salved with very little trouble, and on his leaving me I returned to the dug-out to spend the night.

While Mick was in the line he had attempted to find recruits for the Flying Corps, and despite his description of the antagonistic attitude of the Canadians towards his suggestions, I made up my mind to tempt some of the muddy, begrimed officers. The misery of the underground mud-palace into which I had been invited provided me with sufficient grounds for 'well-meaning' propaganda. The occupants were a Captain and five or six Lieutenants, all stout fellows, accustomed to hardship and danger. To throw our own lives into greater relief against the horror and sordidness of the trenches I extolled the joys of living behind the lines in comfortable billets, eating good food and generally leading a free, unhampered, adventurous life.

At the end of my peroration the Captain poured me out a whisky, then sat down opposite me, straightened the candle and tapped me emphatically on the knee.

"See here, young fellow," he said, "if you think you're going to get any of us to join your corps you're bloody well mistaken. Don't think we haven't seen the dozens of you that have been brought down — killed. When anything goes wrong with you up there you're finished and you've damned well got to wait for it — seeing it staring you in the face before you hit the ground. If we're hit here it's either a 'finish' or a 'Blighty one'. Anyway — we're safe on the ground. No, young mister, we look at the war with older eyes than you, and we don't like seeing you fellows coming down in flames."

I said no more about the joys of being in the Flying Corps.

This brought a murmur of assent from the others, and he continued: "If that's the sort of talk we're going to get from you — you'd better shake hands now while we're still friends, you won't get a chance afterwards."

The next day the mechanics brought a tender to within half a mile of the machine. I was sorry for them, for it meant carting it bit by bit over shell-holes and old German barbed wire, but as I had orders to return to Bruay as soon as possible I had to leave them to their task. Both Davidge and Biggs had had a hard time repairing her and replacing engines. On their arrival at the aerodrome with the machine undamaged I heard that on the day of my departure the place had not only been shelled badly but that the Germans had launched a local gas attack, causing the mechanics to finish the work in gas-masks.

CHAPTER X

ON my return from a second spell of leave at the beginning of December I learnt of the part the Squadron had taken in the Cambrai 'Push'. According to reports in the newspapers this was one of the best-organised attacks in the war. The onslaught on the German lines to the west of Cambrai was carried out with almost complete surprise and, for the first time, both tanks and aircraft were used in close co-operation with the advancing infantry. The main duties of the fighter squadrons were to harass the enemy troops and interrupt their communications; to bomb and attack with machine-gun fire all the strategic positions; to keep the enemy machines from performing similar work on our side of the battle area, and to provide 'intelligence' for the supports.

According to conversations I heard on my return, the Squadron had received the 'Stand by' order on the 19th of November, and after dark the pilots were called to a conference to have their individual duties allotted to them.

To everyone's disappointment the 20th broke with a heavy fog on the ground. Flying was impossible, but later when the heavy wet fog thinned out, machines were able to take off one by one. Several of the younger pilots acquitted themselves well, Wallwork, Wolff, Rusden and Usher, but the outstanding figures of the day were Mannock and Lloyd. Mick, besides carrying out a considerable amount of valuable reconnaissance and troop strafing, had the advantage of flying my machine with its bomb carrier. On each of his trips he was able to drop four 20-pound bombs. Zulu spent every possible minute low down over the enemy territory, harassing the supports, only returning to fill up with petrol and ammunition.

I was very much relieved to find that '40' had suffered no casualties, but Crole (of 43) was missing. There had been no aerial combats, as visibility was too poor for anything but ground work, but despite this the casualties were heavy as a result of the intensive firing that was directed at the machines from the ground. Several days after my return I was pleased to hear that Crole had not been killed but had been taken prisoner, having had his machine shot almost to pieces.

Cambrai was not on 'our' front, it was south of the Scarpe, the southernmost limit of our patrol area, except on special occasions, and as the Germans moved most of their aircraft to the battle area the number on the Armentières-Arras front was decreased. This rendered our patrols more abortive than ever and, feeling that the flight needed 'livening up', Mick frequently led us over Cambrai, but even there we failed to encounter many enemy machines that would offer battle. In furtherance of our policy of guarding as much of the Front as possible, we continued to fly at eighteen thousand to nineteen thousand feet, a miserable job in the cold weather, and before long we were forced to call a conference with a view to restraining Mick. At this time, and in fact from the end of October, Mick and I had shared the flight and a 'roving commission' between us, an arrangement which left us at liberty to do as we pleased and gave us a chance to develop our tactics. The flight had its full complement; with Harrison, McElroy, Learoyd and Wade; and whichever of us — Mick or I — felt in the least belligerent mood took charge of the flight whilst the other acted as 'fairy godmother' or decoy.

Having grown accustomed to the advantages of our fast S.E.5s we were eager to meet some of the enemy formations which, we were informed, No. 56 Squadron were accustomed to engage. Several times we came near the enemy, but although Mick intentionally allowed the Germans to get into position above the level of the flight, the enemy Albatros showed no signs of wanting to attack. On one occasion, seeing that any attempts on my part to climb above the enemy were useless, I made up my mind to try the effect of offering myself as 'bait'. I had never had a 'close in' fight on an S.E.5, and alert and expectant I flew directly underneath the eight enemy machines.

Mick, thinking that the Germans, about whom we had heard so much immediately after 'Cambrai', were sure to nibble at me, 'wagged' his wings to make the flight take up its perfect wing-tip-to-wing-tip formation in readiness for 'rescuing me'. There was no need, however; the Germans were suffering from the cold, and in pure bravado and as a challenge I commenced stunting, rolling and spinning to get them to attack in one of my supposedly unguarded moments. Not even this had any effect, and I seriously considered whether or not I should risk 'looping'. To do so would have meant that on the top of the loop my S.E. would have made an almost stationary target, but the thought of having a hail of incendiary ammunition fired at me while I was upside down prevented what would have been an entirely reckless piece of defiance.

Those Germans would not attack, they spasmodically made half-hearted dives to fire ten or twelve rounds at me, but as their range was two or three hundred yards their smoke streamers never came near. Finally, knowing that we soon would have to go home because the flight's patrol-time was over, I rounded on the Albatros with my Lewis gun, but before I had fired twenty rounds in the direction of the leader all of them pulled up and turned east as quickly as they could.

Mick was so furious at this timorousness that he sent in an indignant report. He would not even be pacified by my explanation that the Germans were the first of the 'fledgelings' and that it was probably the first time they had had 'raw British meat' before them.

On the few days we were able to carry out official patrols we scoured the whole of the front from Douai to Armentières, frequently landing in such a condition that several of us had to be lifted from the machines to restore movement to our stiff and almost frozen legs. Having had less experience of high flying the younger members suffered severely from the cold, and McElroy complained most.

"There's no need to go up so high — you keep below twelve thousand and we'll be all right," I heard him telling Mannock.

McIrish was not easily defeated, and he discovered what he thought was a clever idea of avoiding the results of our high-flying propensities. He sent home for a 'pocket warmer', a small cylindrical tin with smouldering charcoal inside, which would at least keep one part of him warm.

When it arrived McIrish demonstrated it to us with great pride, and before our first patrol he 'chaffed' us about the freezing time that was in store for us. He did not then know what was ahead of *him*.

A pocket warmer may be quite a comfortable gadget in a coat pocket with fairly thin clothing over it but in Mac's trouser pocket, which was covered by the thick sheepskin of his long flying boots and also by the still heavier skin of his fur-lined flying coat, the heat from the charcoal was allowed to accumulate. At first he felt it becoming 'warm', then 'very warm', and as the temperature continued to rise he frantically attempted to remove it.

Unfortunately for him his coat and flying boots prevented him from reaching the pocket, and long before the patrol finished he was in agony.

When we landed, the mechanics lifted him from the machine, and on discovering the trouble we found that the 'pocket warmer' had burnt his leg so badly that there was a blister about the size of a hen's egg.

Mac's 'Patent Pocket Warmer' was a joke in the flight for a long time, and if anyone complained of the cold he was advised to try it.

We afterwards decided to keep our patrols under fourteen thousand feet, and even then the cold was intense. To minimise the effects of the cold and to prevent frostbite we were issued evil-smelling whale oil with which to lubricate our faces and hands. One feature of the high flying I had not forgotten was the weakness of our engines. The higher we were the more secure I felt, the better chance there was of reaching ground on which it was possible to 'land' with some degree of confidence. One extraordinary aspect of these forced landings was that very few of the pilots hurt themselves and, in the majority of cases, the machines were landed without damage. This was remarkable as that ground which was not made unfit by reason of shell-holes, trenches or barbed wire, was mostly under plough.

One evening, when up alone, my engine clanked badly and stopped. I was forced to come down between Mt. St. Eloi and

Houdain. On landing, the machine hit a ridge and tipped up on to her nose. After climbing carefully out of the cockpit, my interest in S.E.5s with dud engines evaporated, and I descended a muddy tree-covered slope to the Arras-Bruay road below.

Sitting down on a stone at the side of the road in the growing darkness and gloom I waited for a lorry or other transport to give me a lift to the aerodrome. Presently a pair of headlights appeared, and on stepping out into the middle of the road to stop the car, to my discomfiture I discovered it was a large limousine.

"Hullo — do you want a lift?" a very pleasant voice called out.

"Yes, Sir," I replied, deeming it wiser to say 'sir' to someone in a limousine with such a voice. "I've had a forced landing and should like the Squadron to know. My machine's on top of the ridge there."

By this time the owner of the voice had opened the door and I saw by his shoulder-straps that he was a General.

On my attempting to apologise for having stopped his car he interrupted me. "Come on, let's see what the damage is."

It began to rain as I led the way up the slippery bank, and when we reached the top and saw the machine the General grunted. "I don't suppose anyone will touch it here in the dark — and the rain. You may as well come with me. You can see about the machine later."

It was no use expostulating with a General, even an Army one, about the impropriety of leaving a machine unprotected, so I followed him in a precipitate descent to the road.

On the way back to Bruay in the comfortable car, during a talk about our S.E.5s I told him of my ideas concerning the withdrawal of the German fighters to act as instructors and the possibility of a large-scale aerial attack in the spring.

"That is more than probable," he remarked, "but you seem to take a great interest in what is happening. You must come to dinner with me at headquarters one night next week."

When I told Mick about this he was furious with me for not taking advantage of the invitation. "There's your chance — a nice 'cushy' job for a few months and then back to the Squadron."

When the car stopped on the road outside the aerodrome I was sorry to leave the comfortable seat and the friendly General. As the difference in our ranks was so great I had not the courage (or effrontery) to ask his name, nor did I have a chance of asking the driver, for immediately the door was closed the car backed on to the aerodrome and drove quickly back along the road towards Houdain.

Soon afterwards Mick and I were speeding along the same road to 'find' the machine. When we ultimately discovered her, Mick decided that as she was out of sight of the road there was no need for a guard and, after covering the already soaked cockpit, we returned to the camp. On the way Mick was silent, he had broken the regulations in not setting a guard for the machine, but, under the circumstances, his consideration for our hard-worked and conscientious mechanics was justified. When he did speak he had obviously been thinking of our crashes.

"It's high time we got out of this before these damned engines kill us," he said bitterly.

The expression of such a thought very often dispels an inner fear, and for a week or so afterwards both of us spent every available hour over the lines, hunting for scouts, and trying to trap the elusive two-seaters.

One of these latter had caused us a good deal of annoyance. From the wireless interception station we discovered that his call sign was GJ, a green and buff-coloured D.F.W. into which both Mick and I had emptied two drums at less than a hundred yards without any apparent effect. One afternoon, however, amidst a steady drizzle, Mick landed. "Got *him* this time, I think. Hit him almost head on, from the front, and he went down — straight."

No one had seen the scrap, and there was no sort of corroboration until the end of the week, when the communique was issued. Mick read it first. "Here, Mac, read this," he said quietly. The report merely stated that on the Monday GJ, who had been transmitting consistently during every fair period, suddenly ceased to transmit and '*had not since been heard*'.

This last clause was accepted by us as evidence that Mick had at last downed our redoubtable enemy. GJ never appeared on the front again.

Most of our skirmishes were with these two-seaters, and one afternoon my own carelessness baulked me of a possible victory. I was 'sitting' at twelve thousand feet several miles on the other side of the line, and although visibility was so poor as to preclude artillery co-operation I saw three two-seaters approaching from the east at nine thousand feet.

Being above them I dived helter-skelter as if to attack the leader from the south, in order to make the observers swing their heavy Spandau guns to that side. Then, depending on my additional speed, I swung round to the east and, before the machine-gunners had time to turn their guns again, fired a burst from my Vickers into the northernmost machine. The Germans continued their westerly course and, dreading the hail from the three guns which had started firing, I dived quickly underneath, letting down my Lewis gun so that I could fire upwards, when — my engine stopped.

Thinking it had been hit I spun for three or four hundred feet to the accompaniment of the pop-popping of the German guns, but as the bullets were wide of their mark I straightened into a steep dive towards the trenches. I was seven or eight miles on the German side of the lines and the wind was against me. The two-seaters made no effort to follow me, and I managed to land safely in a hole on the eastern side of Mazingarbe.

There was no one on the landing ground, and after telephoning to Bruay, I had to wait for Davidge and Biggs to come out to 'rescue' the machine. On their arrival they discovered, very much to their joy and my shame, that there was nothing wrong with the engine. In reaching up to let down my Lewis gun, the strap on my glove had caught in the lever which allowed us to switch over our petrol supply pipe to one of the three tanks and had left it in an 'off' position.

As patrols were becoming fewer and fewer Mannock and I spent every clear hour over the lines, each of us accompanied by one of the others: McElroy, Learoyd or Wade. One afternoon I took Learoyd on a two-seater chasing venture. After passing over Lens we saw two two-seater machines approaching from the east, a little above our level. As the heavy D.F.W.s were not good at manoeuvring I never had any great fear of the pilot's gun, and also because of the observers' inability to fire forward for fear of shooting away their own flying wires, I considered our position was a good one for a determined attack. Signing to Learoyd, who was flying 'wing-tip' with me, to 'cut off' the second machine, I flew straight towards the first one.

The German pilots saw us and closed in just as we attacked. Both of them commenced firing before we were within range, a sure sign the pilots were novices, which relieved me of any fear I had of allowing Learoyd to attack on his own. My confidence was justified, for after attacking my opponent, I saw Learoyd firing the final burst which sent his careering in its last headlong dive.

I did not see what ultimately happened to either of the German machines, but Learoyd had had his first scrap and had proved himself a 'stout fellow'. That was of greater importance to me than the probability that he had actually gained his first victory.

The next day Major Tilney returned from a two days' 'engine course', and as the growth of the Squadron's list of aerial conquests had been retarded so seriously by the bad weather, defective engines, and the absence of potential victims, the C.O. gave a special 'champagne' dinner in honour of the occasion.

At about this time Keen and Lloyd were posted to Home Establishment for a well-deserved rest after the hard fighting of the summer and autumn. The Squadron was sorry to lose them as both had helped a great deal in maintaining the esprit of '40'. Each of them had won the M.C., and although essentially different in 'composition' had proved to be equally courageous. Keen, with his quiet and shy disposition, was nevertheless a determined fighter. He very rarely smiled while, on the other hand, Zulu's face seemed to carry a perpetually good-natured grin. He was quick to act and to say what he thought: one expected brave deeds from Zulu, and got them. No one in the Squadron ever attacked with more persistent ferocity and with such a desire to come to grips. He had been a capable flight commander and had well merited the respect both of his own flight and of the whole Squadron.

Several times I have mentioned this 'respect', but as it was of a type rarely found in civilian life, the realisation of the difference in our conception of character values during a war became of paramount importance. In fighting over the lines our lives were frequently dependent on the courage of our brother pilots, and naturally our best friends were those who stood by us in emergencies. During scraps we had opportunities to observe whether or not the other pilots showed signs of fear or cowardice, whether they possessed that calmly aggressive spirit that made a good fighter, and thirdly, whether they considered the safety of their fellow-pilots above their own glory. During a dog fight in which we were fighting for victory or death it was reassuring to know that if one pilot placed himself in a dangerous position to 'down' one of the enemy, one of the flight would, temporarily, take care that nothing untoward happened.

They say that it is difficult to get people to live together in complete amity even when there is no danger; how much more difficult should it be when living under conditions of almost constantly recurring danger! There was something supremely fine in that mutual respect and trust that one fighter pilot had for the others. Amongst real fighters there was none of the jealousy, snobbery or greed which characterises so-called peaceful pursuits such as business, politics or any of the professions.

Divorced from so-called civilisation we, in the comfort of the Flying Corps, could evaluate each other by the manliness that was in us, by courage, tenacity of purpose, honesty and sympathy. I doubt whether, during my spell in France, I ever heard Mannock or any of the real fighters voice a mean sentiment.

On this account the loss or departure of any of the pilots who had proved himself worthy of our respect and friendship left a gap that was not easily filled.

On our neighbouring front there was much more activity. No. 56 Squadron was doing a considerable amount of damage to the strength and 'morale' of the German 'Jagdstaffeln'. The leading fighter in '56' was McCudden, a friend of Mick's, and one afternoon, when I was painting my machine in an attempt to 'camouflage' the fuselage, Mannock came into the hangar to tell me he wanted me to meet a friend from '56' Squadron. The friend proved to be McCudden, and for a long time we walked up and down the aerodrome discussing S.E.5s and tactics. McCudden was shorter than Mannock, but both his speech and walk had the same determination that marked his fighting career. It was nearly dark when the conversation finished — a most interesting one for me, and McCudden climbed hurriedly into his machine, let the mechanics 'suck in' the engine, gave the self-starter one or two turns, and took off. The S.E.5 had no sooner left the ground than McCudden turned her round on an almost vertical bank, waved to us, and flew off.

"*He's* got faith in his engine!" I remarked. With ours such a take-off with a cold engine would have been almost suicidal.

Mick laughed. "Yes — absolutely confident. He's a good fellow, young Mac, one of the best."

'56' had had very little trouble with their engines, but forced landings continued to plague us.

One of my own happened under peculiar circumstances. I was leading the flight towards the line when my radiator began to steam. The oil pressure gauge had dropped to zero, and there was no alternative to firing my green light and returning to the aerodrome. Fearing I might not reach it I kept the engine running at about half-speed, attempting to force the radiator fins open to their fullest extent in the hope that the engine would not seize up.

As the machine, now belching clouds of steam, came within gliding distance of the aerodrome, I switched off, but to my disgust the cylinder heads were so hot that the engine kept on running as if at half-throttle. Nothing proved of any avail, and a real predicament faced me. The machine could not possibly stay up, nor could I land her with even a reasonable chance of avoiding a crash, and the wind was blowing from the hangars to the aerodrome.

My speed was between seventy and eighty miles an hour, and at five hundred feet I realised that it would indeed require a desperate effort to save myself, far less the machine. Only then I remembered the four bombs underneath the fuselage.

Turning so that the machine would have the full length of the aerodrome to run, I touched the ground at the south-west corner, but as she showed no signs of losing speed I was faced with the alternatives of running straight into the house at the corner, charging the hangar with, possibly, mechanics inside, or of allowing a row of Sopwith 'Camels' to arrest my progress.

Although it all happened in a second or two the crash was perfectly premeditated. At about twenty yards from the end machine full left rudder caused my right wing to hit the ground and crumple up and, wiping her undercarriage off, the remains of the machine slithered round and charged the 'Camels', bowling the first one right over and finishing up amidst the wreckage of the second. The impact was so great that the buckled bomb carrier released the bombs, none of which exploded, fortunately. What was more disconcerting for the onlookers was the row made by my Lewis gun as it emptied a whole drum of ammunition into the ground. The crash had tightened the wire sufficiently to fire the gun.

This took place inside a cloud of steam from the burst radiator, which created the impression that the machine was on fire. Two or three valiant mechanics who dashed into the mix-up to the rescue, found me disentangling myself. I had not suffered even a scratch.

The Sopwith Camels belonged to an Australian flight that had just landed *en route* for the Ypres front, and when I was in the ante-room writing a humble apology to the Australian commanding officer for destroying his machines, Mannock remonstrated with some of the others who were disturbing *him.* "Shut up, you fellows, can't you see Mac's writing an essay on 'how to crash three machines in one landing'?"

Next day orders arrived to the effect that my bomb carrier was to be removed, but as it had afforded me so much 'amusement' and the longerons of my fuselage were not broken, the machine was rebuilt with the repaired bomb carrier in position.

This crash had a depressing influence on Mick. On the following Sunday afternoon, sitting in the warmth of the ante-room and listening to the rain outside, I called his attention to Wolff, who was lying back in one of the arm-chairs. The young pilot was pale and his head was swaying slightly as if he were just going to fall asleep. He had crashed badly into a haystack on the range that morning, because of engine failure; and the impact had given him slight concussion.

Mick watched Wolff for a few moments then turned to me: "If that big push you talk about is 'coming off' in the spring, the sooner we get our three months' rest the better. They may have good engines for us by that time."

His highly strung nervous temperament required periods of activity separated by short spells of complete repose, but during December he was allowed to have neither. The huts were too cold to allow him to take his wonted hours of sleep during the day; and the ante-room, our enforced home, was too noisy, had too many distractions — Pontoon, Bridge, Poker and 'yarns'. Even the C.O., who had other distractions such as polo, squash, and frequent excursions to dine with friends, was affected by our depression.

Mannock's bitterness boiled over one day just before Christmas. Through engine failure he had had to land in the old German trenches to the southeast of Souchez amongst the now bare skeletons of the Canadian and German dead, and after spending five or six hours in a steady drizzle without food and without even a cigarette, while the mechanics were trying to locate him, he returned to the camp, angry, disgusted and dejected.

After dinner, noticing that he had left the mess, I went to his hut where I found him sitting on his bed, one hand on each knee, swinging backwards and forwards. His face was wrought with misery, and at each forward movement of his body he let out a prolonged groan.

I had seen him doing this before, a form of Irish 'keening' in which the 'mourner' reviles fate for taking away a beloved friend. He had done it after Kennedy's death, moaning: "Ah, Ken, why did you die!"

This time, however, the tears were in his eyes and he groaned without saying anything.

"Here — stop it," I said.

After a few more heaves he stopped and looked at me, unashamed of the tears in his eyes.

"It's a miserable life, Mac. Do you know, there's only one bright spot in the whole of my existence out here."

"Come on, into the mess, or to Bethune," I said, knowing that I had to save him from this mood.

He pulled himself together, wiped his eyes. "I mean it," he said, "only one bright spot, old Mac. I'll give you three guesses and you won't find it."

To humour him I thought for a moment and said: "I know, you old blighter" — pointing to my head as he had done when he told me about it — "three little bullet holes in a Hun's head."

My imitation made him smile. "No; I've forgotten all that now. No, Mac, the only kindness of heart I have had out here I will never forget — when you bought this bit of ribbon and sewed it on my tunic."

I knew then that it was high time he had a rest at home; he had been fighting for nine months, beating the Germans and conquering himself. The strain was beginning to 'break' him. His ambition to prove his worth even to himself had gone, his object had been achieved, he was flight commander with the M.C. and bar, but his only longing was for the affection and loyalty of friendship. His desires had turned a complete somersault.

This was the result of his moral and physical tiredness. Health and strength had given him ambition; now, his sickening nerves were making him crave for sympathy. There were three types of fighter, the hard-headed, unimaginative fellow who regarded fighting as he would a desperate game; the emotional fighter who, carried away by his own enthusiasm both for the cause, and in a spirit of self-assertion, behaved in an irresponsible reckless manner; and the level-headed, thoughtful fighter, perfectly conscious of the issues at stake, who used his intelligence and imagination to develop himself as a fighter. Mick belonged to this last category, and because of the conflict that had taken place within him, the diffidence and lack of assurance that had characterised his first efforts, and the quickness with which he surmounted all the obstacles after he had taken the first hurdle, any retrogression in his mental outlook would have entirely destroyed the spirit from which his success had sprung. Self-pity is akin to conceit, but in Mick's case it revealed to me that, despite the success of which he had every reason to be proud, his soul was becoming bared to the acid emptiness of life.

His tense nerves almost persuaded him that something was about to happen, and on several occasions he brought up the subject of catching fire in the air.

It happened that at the same time the same dread often assailed me, and one day, hearing me asking the mechanics to empty out my emergency tank, he was horrified to hear my reason.

"When I was up in the dusk the other evening," I said, "I saw the flames shooting out of the exhausts, and in case that tank is hit 1 don't want any petrol near the flames." The small emergency tank was built into the centre-section, forming part of the top planes, and any puncture would, in certain circumstances, have allowed the petrol to drop on the exhausts which ended on either side of the cockpit.

"So you are thinking about that too," he said when I had explained how easily it could take place.

I was ashamed of having given voice to this fear, realising that it was but the outcome of the nervous strain of fighting and forced landings, but when the mechanics had gone into the hangar Mick cheered up.

"Then you won't mind going home with me?"

This seemed to be almost an obsession with him, that he and I were going together, although I had been only seven months with the Squadron. He looked forward to our returning to France. "When they are coming over in twenties and thirties in this big push of yours we'll get all the fighting we want."

On Christmas Day there was a steady drizzle and, in case Jerry was not bearing in mind the goodwill that was supposed to descend on the brutalised, soul-sickening countryside, one flight spent an hour patrolling on our side of the lines. On their return the hangars were shut up and the Squadron settled down to the quiet enjoyment of 'Christmas at the Front'.

The humbug of it all offended me. 'Goodwill to all men!' with corpses rotting in the trenches; wounded in the hospitals; gas compressed in cylinders ready to tear the lungs to pieces; shells stacked near the guns to blast the already shattered houses and troops; bombs lying in the stores waiting to be dropped on defenceless civilians; and machine-gun belts already filled for the genteel and humane destruction of the enemy; the thought of all of these showed me the mockery of it, the deep-rooted paganism that called on us one day to kill for our country's sake, and on the next expected us to hold fire in reverence for a tradition.

Having in me a fundamental belief in the humanity and martyrdom of Christ, the Christlessness of the whole battlefront, of the churches at home that prayed for the destruction of the enemy just as the Kaiser claimed divine right on his side, filled me with disgust at the unreality of the whole hypocritical edifice that had been constructed around what we called our civilisation.

I made up my mind that for me at least the war would not cease on Christmas Day, and after lunch I was putting on my heavy flying boots when Mick came to my hut to ask me to make a fourth at Bridge.

"What on earth are you doing? You aren't going up?" he asked.

"Yes. I've got no belief in this goodwill. We're still at war, and I mean to do a bit extra as it's Christmas Day."

Mick's susceptibilities were offended, and for some time he argued with me that as fighting — or even killing — was our work, and work was supposed to cease on Christmas Day, it was my duty to remain on the ground.

"Well, in any case, I'm going up the line to make sure that Fritz isn't up to any mischief."

"All right then, I'll walk round to the hangar with you," he said. Thoroughly well wrapped up and with my face and hands smothered in whale oil, I walked beside him — silent because he was thinking.

As we approached the hangar he stopped:

"But look here, Mac — you aren't going up to-day! Don't tell me you're serious?"

"Of course I am," I said, and pushing open the flaps of the hangar stepped inside and called Davidge and Biggs.

Mick realised how serious I was when he heard me asking the mechanics to fit four high explosive bombs to the rack.

He had no coat, but in spite of a drizzle that was falling, he followed me out to my machine when the mechanics had brought it out.

When I was tucked into the cockpit he leant over me. "All right — good luck to you." He was surprisingly cheery.

My two mechanics, with raincoats on, 'sucked in' the engine, called, "Contact, Sir." I turned the starting magneto, but no answering 'kick' came from the cylinders. Many times we repeated the attempt without success and, after emptying out the carburettor, the mechanics tried again — also without result.

At length the Sergeant came over to me. "Captain Mannock's compliments, Sir," he said, "will you join him in a drink in our mess. It will give the mechanics a chance."

The sergeants' mess was in an estaminet just across the road from 'A' flight hangar and, when I entered, Mick was sitting at the table talking earnestly to two or three of the sergeants.

"What will you drink, Mr. Mac?" one of them asked. "Captain Mick refuses to have anything but a grenadine. You'll have something decent."

"A very small one then," I answered, "I'm just going up."

171

They gave me a whisky, and I sat down, still wearing my flying coat which was dripping with rainwater.

Mannock kept the conversation rolling for some time, but at length one of the sergeants advised me to take off my wet coat. Only then I realised it was nearly dark and, on looking over to the aerodrome to find out what the mechanics were doing, I saw that the hangar had been shut up. There was no sign of my machine.

As I turned round impatiently, there was a loud roar of laughter — except from Mick who was examining the pottery mark on a plate very intently. I immediately appreciated that I had been the victim of a practical joke. The Flight Sergeant then told me that there had never been any possibility of my taking the machine up as, *on Captain Mannock's orders*, my self-starter had been disconnected.

CHAPTER XI

ON Boxing Day it became evident to me that Mick had another practical joke in preparation. He pretended to show an unusual consideration for my health, telling me to eat lots of good food, offering me the most sheltered seat in the mess and generally behaving as if I were an invalid.

Puzzled, I left him to work out his joke to his own satisfaction.

The next morning while I was dressing, rather late for breakfast, Dr. Cranston came to the door of my hut.

"Good morning, Mac. Why are you getting up?"

"There isn't anything wrong with me — why?" I replied.

'Crannie' was one of the most sympathetic and popular of the Wing Staff, and, as our respect for him was similar of our reverence for Padre Keymer, I asked him into the hut, glad to have the opportunity of a talk.

"I heard you were ill," he remarked. "If you are, why are you getting up on a day like this?"

"No, I'm perfectly fit, but what sort of joke is this; who told you to come to me?"

His refusal to tell me made me surmise that Mick had been the culprit, and when I said so the doctor's expression confirmed my conjecture.

" I've come to examine you, and may as well 'run over' you," he said, tapping his pocket from which the ear pieces of his stethoscope were protruding.

Very tactfully I refused to remove my underclothes to be examined, and the doctor sat talking until I had finished dressing.

Filled with curiosity and indignation at Mick's perfidy I hurried into the mess to look for him.

The others had finished breakfast, and Mick was sitting on one of the settles next the fire, talking to Harrie, Learoyd and Wolff. Something in my appearance told him that I had found him out.

As usual he attempted to pass it off as a joke and to side-track the issue in his own spontaneous way. He grabbed Harrison and Learoyd by the arms and held them together in front of him, yelling, "Kamerad, Kamerad, McIrish, Wade, save me; Mac's after my skin."

Such a beginning frequently resulted in a 'rag' but, as I had not had breakfast, and, knowing there was something behind Mick's action, I refused the 'bait' and, sitting down on the corner of the card-table, demanded:

"Why did you send 'Crannie' to me?"

Mick shot both arms into the air and again yelled "Kamerad", and as an afterthought, "McIrish, Learoyd, Wade, Harrie — off the ground at two-thirty pip emma, Mac says it, he's in a bloodthirsty mood."

"Yes; but that doesn't answer my question, why —" He let me get no further.

"We're going to find some nice fat juicy Huns for you this afternoon; that will make you forget about Crannie!"

It was impossible to be annoyed with him for any length of time, and as Sergeant Simmonds came to the door to remind me that if I delayed much longer I would have to go without breakfast, I had to repair to the dining-room, leaving Mick to chuckle over my discomfiture.

Sometimes Mick showed an almost childish cunning, and I was more than ever persuaded that he had had some definite object in calling in the Wing Doctor.

After lunch the weather was almost unfit for flying, not the type of day we could expect to meet Germans. Instead of one of us going off on our own, Mick and I decided to go with the whole flight, six machines. Mick was leading, with Learoyd and Wade beside him, Harrie and McElroy behind these, while I brought up the rear, between the latter two.

There was a wetting mist near the ground, and above it, at eight thousand feet, was a heavy bank of clouds. When we ascended above that we saw another mountainous layer of cumulus clouds at fifteen thousand feet. We crossed the lines between the two banks of cloud, and as there were no enemy machines in sight Mick climbed through the upper layer.

We emerged from the bitterly cold cloud into a world of glittering white iciness. The sun was shining brilliantly and a glistening expanse of white hills of powdered snow appeared before us as a newly created world. The reflected light from the clouds was blinding, and as the surfaces of the 'hummocks' and slopes were clearly defined, the silhouettes of our machines showed up with almost perfect definition, each one surrounded by a circular halo of rainbow colours.

On every side of us the clouds stretched right to the horizon, the intense whiteness of those farthest away bearing testimony to the crystal purity of the atmosphere. It was indeed an entrancing world in which our S.E.s were suspended, and very soon the rest of us realised that it had cast its spell over Mick. The wild loneliness had roused his boyish spirits. There were no other machines in sight, the world was ours, and Mick 'wagged' his wings once, asking us to take up our wing-tip-to-wing-tip formation and, without giving the second 'waggle' that would have signified the presence of an enemy, dived slowly towards the clouds.

He flattened out just above them and began contour-chasing amongst the steep feathery mountains and valleys, round one peak, down the slopes into a hollow, zooming up to avoid the next mountain, occasionally dashing into an overhanging precipice of freezing cold, billowing cloud, all the time with the silent rainbow spectres following us or preceding us as we turned and twisted over the arctic expanse.

In the thrilling excitement of flying in such exceptionally magnificent circumstances, and following a leader with such an appreciation of the beautiful and glorious scenery, we all entered into the spirit of the chase, forgetting the war in our enjoyment.

On and on we went, six dark shapes skimming over a fairyland, heedless of whither we were going. It was cold, not a shivering damp cold, but a clear, empty chill that made my bones feel light, and as each successive plunge through the edge of a cloud left another rough layer of freezing, opalescent ice on the front of my planes and on the ailerons I began to fear that if we continued much longer our controls would freeze completely.

Mick evidently saw the danger and attempted to throw the ice from his planes by wagging his wings but, failing to make any effect on it, he dived almost vertically through the clouds.

Bringing up the rear, I had the additional pleasure of seeing the machines of the others meeting their respective silhouettes and throwing columns of whirling 'steam-like' foam into the air as they hit the surface.

Leaving our glorious sunlit world we descended into the dull region between the two layers and, continuing the dive, we emerged from the lower bank about fifteen miles on the German side of the lines.

Soon Archie got our range, a harsh reminder of the war. There were no hostile machines to be seen, and as making ourselves targets for the anti-aircraft gunners at that dangerous height would have been silly, Mick climbed above the lower bank of clouds and flew westwards.

When we landed his face was beaming with joy. Whether at work, play, or paying compliments to the fair sex, the whole of his vital enthusiasm was directed towards the immediate object. Our entrancing flight in the solitude and beauty of the upper air had stirred him, as it had thrilled us.

Evening fell clear and frosty, and after a cheery dinner in Bethune, Mick and I returned to camp full of hope and vigour. 'A' flight was in admirable trim, Harrie, Learoyd, McElroy and Wade were all stout fellows, and Mick was more than ever confident.

The next morning was frosty and sunny, and although there was no official patrol for us, I decided to take the flight over the lines. Both Mick and I were confident the Germans would appear on such a beautiful morning. Learoyd, McElroy, Wade and Harrie were as keen as we, and, tossing up to see whether Mick or I should lead the flight, it fell to my lot.

Just before I took off Mick came to my machine; "You'll get all the fighting you want this morning. I'm going to sit up above and watch you. — Join you over the lines," he said, just as if we were starting on a picnic.

We had made our arrangements before leaving the ground, and flying tip-to-tip with Learoyd and Wade and McElroy and Harrie behind them in a close 'V' formation, we crossed the lines at ten thousand feet. In the far east there were several bunches of 'specks', obviously German machines, as there were no signs of Archie bursts amongst them. Deeming it wiser to climb higher into the sun before heading for them, we flew south to the Scarpe, then turned south-east towards Cambrai, still climbing.

The Germans (there were as far as I could see about thirty of them) were quietly manoeuvring towards the lines between La Bassée and Vimy. Confident that the majority of them had not seen us getting 'into the sun on them' I flew northwards, keeping a close look out for any that might have escaped my notice in our rear. There was something stealthy in the way we stalked them, the whole atmosphere seemed tense, a feeling which was possibly heightened by the absence of anti-aircraft firing.

The Germans, mostly single-seater Albatros, separated into flights, several of these heading north, while three flights, one of three and two of six machines, turned south in our direction, two thousand feet below our level. The smaller flight was uppermost, and as such an opportunity was too good to be lost, despite the superior numbers of the enemy, I determined to attack the three and to zoom up again before attacking the others. The three Albatros were painted white, probably winter camouflage, and as I wagged my wings, Learoyd, Wade, McIrish and Harrie closed in and wagged excitedly in reply. Waiting a few seconds I wagged again and, firing a few rounds from each gun, dived hell-for-leather at the leading Albatros just as they, evidently sensing danger, turned east.

This was one of the moves we had anticipated in our practice and, having confidence in the flight, I swung round quickly and fired fifty rounds into the Albatros, which 'dived' down almost vertically. Learoyd tackled another, and as I flattened out, Wade's machine almost hit my Lewis gun. Then I caught sight of one of our machines flying straight into the lower flight of six Germans.

There was a 'mix-up' immediately and, closely followed by the others, I dived into it, seeing a machine, an Albatros, spinning down out of control. The S.E. was still there and, thinking more of safeguarding the reckless member of the flight than of attacking the Germans, I fired here and there as the Albatros came into line with my machine-gun. The majority seemed only intent on getting away from us, but I saw one sitting above, waiting for his chance to fire. No sooner had his nose gone down towards the S.E. than I let down my Lewis gun and, desperately anxious to prevent his hitting one of the flight, emptied the whole drum at about a hundred and fifty yards' range. The tracer seemed to spray all over the Albatros, which continued to dive but did not fire.

Much quicker than it had taken us to get into the fight, the Germans disappeared, and to my great joy all our machines fell in behind me, and a minute later we were joined by Mick who flew directly above me.

He 'wagged' his wings and pointed to the north where we saw another fight in progress, but before we could reach them the Germans had flown eastwards with their 'noses well down' — to join a few more 'specks' which were flying at five or six thousand feet ten miles on their side of the lines.

Afraid that the clear weather might necessitate an official patrol for which we would be unprepared I thought it advisable to return to Bruay, and, on signing my intention to Mick, he also turned west with us, and we threaded our way back through clouds of bursts from the angry Archie gunners.

On landing, my first question to the others was to find out which of them had attacked the twelve Albatros. McIrish was the culprit, and after hearing my opinion of his courage, his success and his *lack* of discipline, he was attempting to defend his action by saying: "I thought you meant to attack the lot the way you swung round," when Mick climbed out of his machine.

"Which of you was it?"

"Mac," I said, and McElroy waited, expecting some praise from his fellow-countryman.

There was a lively twinkle in Mick's eyes as he said:

178

"What do you think our Pygmalion duty is, to risk our lives protecting you, you hot-headed Irish spalpeen? You might have lost Mac the whole blinking flight. Couldn't you wait to see what Mac was going to do?"

Poor McElroy, he did not know now whether we were serious or not, and only after having filled in our reports did I congratulate him on his first 'blood'. There was no doubt that the Albatros had gone down to its destruction. Mick then gave him a severe lecture on tactics and flight policy — telling him that against fourteen of the enemy we should really have had little chance in a dog-fight.

"Remember, McIrish, none of us want to see you 'go' as you certainly will if you behave in that high-blooded Irish way of yours. You leave it to your leader. The flight might have had half a dozen of them if you hadn't split them up."

The mess was lively that day, for two other pilots were able to claim victories, and everyone in the Squadron had been engaged in a fight of some sort. Mick openly showed his pride in 'A' flight.

Later in the day I heard him conveying the enthusiasm to the flight sergeants.

"It was the finest show I've seen, and not one of them had a bullet hole."

It was encouraging for me, the others had *seen* everything that had happened, and I looked forward to leading them on still more profitable ventures.

Two days later, however, Mick came to the door of my hut, his 'old time' grin covering his rugged countenance. Holding out a yellow ticket he said: "Got my ticket, old boy. Home to good old Blighty and then back for the big fight!"

I was momentarily relieved, and laughed at him for having suggested that I was going home too.

"Don't you worry, Mac; you're coming with me: your ticket is round there as well. They wouldn't give it to me. We've only got forty-eight hours to get out of France, and we'll be together still."

I did not quite share his joy. Our inactivity which had resulted from the weather and engine trouble was no fit climax

179

to a spell of service even although it might be but the training prelude to still greater activity. I felt cheated.

"But that's damned unfair. I've only been out seven months," I said bitterly. "I'm going to have it out with the new Wing Commander."

"Not the slightest use, old boy." Mick laughed, relishing the joke he had played on me. "You're going home on medical grounds — you're cracking up — that's why Crannie wanted to examine you, because I told them. If you come quietly now we can stick together till the end. We'll be back for the big fight." We had no intention of taking advantage of our warrants and, next morning, we decided to carry out a final 'strafe'. The weather was miserable, and as it did not seem likely that we should encounter any enemy aircraft I had my full complement of bombs fitted to the rack and three drums of armour piercer for the Lewis gun placed in the holders. The bombs were for the Cambrai-Douai railway, and the armour piercer ammunition for the Germans in the trenches. We had noticed a good deal of activity on the railway which connected the Ypres front with Cambrai, and all that had prevented my bombing trains had been dread of an inopportune engine failure.

This morning the temptation to have a last destructive raid against the enemy was strong. My luck was 'in', for after contour-chasing to Douai I dropped my bombs from two hundred feet, getting direct hits on the tracks, after which I returned to empty my ammunition into the German trenches.

Mick's trip was even more fortunate. Taking his usual beat between Lens and Henin Lietard, he met a two-seater and shot it down into our trenches. It was the first day of the year, Mick had begun well.

That evening there was a quiet farewell dinner:

Huitres Natives, Potage de Fampoux,

Carrelets Fritz, *Boeuf Roti au* Ration,

Asperges en branches, Fruits de Bruay,

Bambouches ties Heraldes, Dessert. Café.

Combined with Lady Killers and champagne it was a merry meal, at the end of which Major Tilney made a blushing speech. He spoke in most glowing terms of Mick's courage and of his ability as a flight commander.

The next morning, when our forty-eight hours had elapsed, I was helping Finlay to pack my belongings when the feeling of having been thwarted again returned. I went to Mick's hut where he too was in the midst of his packing.

"What about a last 'go' at them?" I asked.

"That's an idea, I wonder if we can risk it. What time is the tender coming for us?"

"Two o'clock."

It was then almost eleven, and we hurried to the aerodrome.

Mick's machine was nearest the entrance to the hangar, and by the time Davidge and Biggs were getting mine out Mick had revved his engine and was taking off.

The sound of a machine leaving the ground drew Major Tilney's attention from squadron affairs, and as I was about to climb into my S.E. he came over from the orderly-room.

"Look here, Mac, you can't go up, you're already struck off the strength."

"Hang it all, Major. Mick's just gone up. I'm to meet him over the lines," I said.

"But neither of you has any right to have a machine."

We argued about it for two or three minutes, finally agreeing that as mine was the most valuable machine in the Squadron, because of my extra 'gadgets', official anger might be mollified if I took the worst machine, Harrison's, the machine on which we had all learnt to fly S.E.5s.

Having been deprived of a bomb carrier, a low strafe would have been futile, so I climbed towards the lines and headed for Henin Lietard. The air was fairly clear and in the distance I sighted a D.F.W. flying westwards.

Harrie's machine that day seemed to find the 'ceiling' at seventeen thousand feet, so that any attempt to get between the D.F.W. and the sun was hopeless. I flew straight towards the enemy, and at a quarter of a mile the pilot caught sight of me and turned back. Although the range was too long I fired both guns at the retreating Germans 'without apparent effect', as they continued on their course. Letting down my Lewis gun to change the drum I noticed that the oil pressure gauge was registering zero and, being several miles on the German side of the lines, I turned back.

About half-way to Bruay the water in the radiator began to boil. The engine did not seize, but, puffing steam, Harrie's S.E.5, hissing and clanking, carried me back to the aerodrome — a fitting farewell to S.E.5s with dud engines.

After a hurried lunch Mick came to me.

"Do me a favour, Mac. I've got a Canadian friend come over to see me and I want to see some people on the way to Boulogne. Try to wangle it so that you go in the Squadron car and I in the tender. You go off first."

As almost everyone wanted to take a trip to Boulogne I had no difficulty in arranging the car-loads as he suggested.

When we left, the whole ground personnel of the Squadron lined the aerodrome to bid us farewell. They cheered lustily as the tender passed, and looking back at them, I felt a wave of emotion surge over me. Our cheery family, 'A' flight, had been my school; the mechanics and N.C.O.s had done everything possible to make 'their' pilots safe and happy; Davidge and Biggs would, the next day, be attending to another pilot's machine, my S.E.5. Bitterness against our miserable engines was almost forgotten.

When we met Mick in Boulogne he was in a boisterous mood, and as none of the others had any right to be in Boulogne we dined in a small select restaurant off the main street, evidently a 'hide' where staff officers could arrange clandestine meetings with W.A.A.C. girls and nurses.

Mick and I shared a room at the Hôtel de Louvre, and as the first boat, on which we hoped to embark without being noticed because we were a day late, left at 9.30, we had to get up early.

Breakfast in the Squadron had always been a rather meagre meal on account of the scarcity of porridge and bacon and, having dressed first, I was demolishing a plate of bacon with two eggs when Mick joined me.

I remarked on the excellence of the porridge, but Mick remonstrated: "Don't mention the word, the Channel is as rough as blazes, and I confess I'm the world's worst sailor."

After having seen him performing all types of voluntary and involuntary evolutions in the air, it came as a great surprise to hear that he suffered from sea-sickness. I laughed heartily at the diffident way he nibbled his *petit-pain* and butter.

He laughed too. "Yes, you'll beat me hollow to-day."

We sat at a table with an R.F.C. officer who had been in Switzerland having some form of treatment. He was in civilian clothes, and after a few cautious replies from me (we were always on our guard against inquisitive strangers, particularly civilians), he committed the usual 'crime'.

"How many Germans have you brought down?"

CONCLUSION

AS everyone knows, the 'big push' by the Germans actually commenced in March 1918. For their final desperate effort to break through our lines towards Paris and the Channel ports they brought forward all their resources, including the many hundreds of pilots they had been training during the winter. To consolidate any victories obtained on the ground it was essential that they should also be victorious in the air.

Although their well-organised infantry made such material advances on their objectives that in April 1918 General Haig felt justified in sending forth his 'back-to-the-wall' manifesto, the German Jagdstaffeln (pursuit flights) failed to make much impression on the formidable barrier of fighting squadrons that had been brought up in support of our defence measures.

The Germans once more attempted to wrest the air supremacy from the R.F.C. but, despite the fact that their factories had been under contract to supply two thousand aeroplanes per month and the number of flights of fighter machines (of fourteen aeroplanes each) was doubled, they failed in their aerial objective as they did, ultimately, on the ground.

In preparation for this the German War Office, which throughout the war had shown such precision and astuteness in their organisation, had withdrawn much of the badly needed financial support from the mechanised arms, such as tanks, in favour of the still more urgent requirements of a competent air force. The German General Staff had been quick to appreciate that the continuance of our air supremacy, besides being of great practical utility to our infantry, artillery and intelligence, was likely to prove a potent factor in the demoralisation of their own forces.

It could not have been an encouraging sight for the German troops, seeing our machines patrolling miles on their side of the lines, and observing that in almost every combat our pilots took up the offensive.

Summing up the position in 1917: the German two-seaters were rarely able to carry out their essential work, such as artillery co-operation, bombing or photographic reconnaissance; or at least their activities were so seriously curtailed because of our tactics as to render their work almost valueless. On our side, the two-seaters were seen confidently patrolling up and down over the lines, registering for the artillery; our bombing and photographic machines penetrated far into enemy territory, doing considerable damage to important communications and returning with photographs which showed clearly any increase of activity or equipment that might give warning of an impending German attack. In addition there was the efficient contact patrol work carried out by squadrons similar to '43' during infantry attacks, and the balloon strafing and harassing of ground troops and transport by our single-seater fighters.

These evidences of our 'supremacy' in the air in 1917 had justified the enemy's decision to utilise everything at their disposal to make a success of the intended attack in 1918.

Those of us who had interpreted the signs correctly — the withdrawing of the experienced fighters to train the horde of new pilots in the art of war, the quick appearances and disappearances of apparently inexperienced flights on our sector of the front, and the obvious lack of desire on the part of these flights to risk encounters with our fighters — hoped that similar preparations were being made on our side.

Mick and I, having been posted to Home Establishment at the same time so that we might remain together, confidently expected to be posted to some training squadron of single-seater fighters or, better still, to a complete unit which would in due course be posted to France as a squadron. Instead, much to our annoyance and disappointment, Mannock was sent to an experimental wireless school at Biggin Hill to fly F.E.2.B.s, a job which could have been undertaken by any one of the hundreds of ex-schoolboys who had just qualified, or by disabled or inefficient pilots; while I was sent to a home defence squadron to fly B.E.12s, machines which were obsolete by the end of 1916 and which had no hope of entering into combat with the German bombers.

Events happened which prevented my returning to France; but Mick, finding himself relegated to a backwater where he was likely to remain until the end of the war, agitated for a transfer so violently, and was so outspoken in his condemnation of the lack of intelligent organisation on the part of the authorities, that, braving court-martial, he succeeded in getting a transfer to No. 74 Training Squadron.

No. 74 had been formed by Major Dore of '43', and was intended to form a new unit for overseas. Soon after Mick's joining it, the command was given to Major Caldwell of '60', one of our sister Nieuport Squadrons, and both Mannock and Caldwell undertook the actual 'fighting training' of the new pilots. Mick was in his element, and with the energetic support of Major 'Grid' Caldwell he helped to build up one of the most efficient fighting units that ever went to France.

Training novices is one of the most pleasant tasks anyone can undertake when the instructor knows the subject thoroughly and the pupils are receptive. Before leaving 40 Squadron Mick's quick intelligence had grasped the essential features of aerial warfare; the psychology, tactics and spirit that were demanded from those who wished to make themselves efficient in their jobs. He knew that our aerial supremacy had been maintained not by superior numbers, for these could be, to a great extent, discounted because of the inferiority of our machines, but by the spirit, determination and intelligence of the pilots. He therefore enlightened the pilots on the psychological reactions they were likely to feel, the types of enemy they would encounter, and the tactics they should employ. Above all, he tried to imbue his listeners with the spirit that would turn them into fighters.

How well he succeeded may be judged by the record of '74'.

The Squadron went overseas and took up its fighting duties at the time when Haig issued his now famous 'back-to-the-wall' order. On the ground the Germans had made important advances towards getting a stranglehold on our communications, and both on the ground and in the air it behoved every fighter to utilise his entire energy to save our armies from defeat. The Germans were desperate — it was their last hope — but our defences were proving inadequate to meet the onslaught. Everyone, at least every rational patriot, knew that there was only one British characteristic that had not been utilised to its fullest extent — the indomitable spirit that makes us refuse to recognise defeat when it appears on the horizon.

It was almost too late, as usual, before the people at headquarters and at home realised this. Mannock, and all those who had taken a real interest and had played an active part in the waging of the war in 1917, knew how much we could rely on this spirit. It had been Mick's doctrine in lecturing his new pupils, and the results of their work can best be summarised in the record of their squadron — 221 enemy machines shot down in a little over seven months, with the loss of 16 killed, 3 wounded and 5 taken prisoner. By June, Mannock himself had brought down over forty.

Haig's manifesto, which caused consternation and almost panic at home, had the desired effect in France. There were tens of thousands of fighters who, by a wholehearted effort, stemmed the German advance on the ground while, in the air, thanks to the policy pursued by II.Q. in giving the lead to fellows like Mannock, the enemy never even approached equality in the aerial war. Despite their advantages the enemy were forced to fight even over their own aerodromes. Mannock carried on the spirit of his saying on the memorable morning when 'Bud's machine was set on fire: "We'll chase the Huns out of *our* sky." As flight commander and leader of a whole squadron he continued his patrols far into enemy territory, keeping the sky clear for our reconnaissance and observation machines and teaching the enemy that in the air, at least, they were no match for our fighters.

Readers who had no experience of the war, or who are unaware of the causes of a great deal of friction during a war, may be puzzled as to why I have laid particular emphasis on the *spirit* epitomised so definitely in Mannock's career.

During a war the conflict between the man of action and the academician is even more acute than in times of peace or in civilian occupations. Unfortunately, a great deal of training for war has to be undertaken from the purely scholastic point of view, and those who get into positions of authority, to a very great extent, are those who have shown the greatest reverence for the prejudices inseparable from all scholastic educations.

Whenever a war breaks out different qualities are demanded: independence of thought, originality, deductive reasoning as opposed to inductive, and personal courage as opposed to collective or herd security. These form the principal characteristics of the typical man of action — the ordinary, reasoning, confident, hard-working fellow who is prepared to take off his coat when the occasion demands.

At the battlefront men of action are required in all forces: infantry, artillery, transport and above all in the Air Force. In 1914 the infantry looked with scorn on the beginnings of the Flying Corps, and many generals held out no prospect of success for what they considered a useless arm.

The Corps, being new, and having been formed merely as a 'rib' of the army, was first nurtured on 'Infantry Training', regardless whether or no any detail of infantry warfare could be remotely compared with war as it was to develop in the air. Worse even than this was the supposition that the same psychological attributes were required from an 'air pilot' as from the infantryman who had been reared on the 'Theirs not to reason why' principle.

The R.F.C. from 1914 to 1916 *required individualists*. The pilots were almost free to do as they wished, working out their own collaboration with the other forces, infantry, or artillery, even to the extent of devising their own gun mountings and signalling codes for communicating with troops or gunners. Before long, however, some definite standardisation was required, and the 'individualists', as they were scathingly called, were developed into an organised unit with separate squadrons each allotted its specialised duties, such as I have described in No. 2, No. 25, No. 43 and No. 40, which can be regarded as typical squadrons.

There was, and still is, a recognised presumption that the individualist or 'lone hand' is never any use in an organised unit; but those who were thoroughly cognisant of affairs in the R.F.C. and the work that had to be done knew how utterly false this was.

Discipline of the 'spit-and-polish' variety was almost entirely lacking, and any officer who had been steeped in infantry training to such an extent that his mind could not conceive anything different, received scant courtesy at the hands of the fighting squadrons in France. This was made obvious in the number of senior officers who failed to adapt themselves to the conditions under which we had to work, and who were, therefore, returned to Home Establishment where their rigid discipline and 'hot air' could have full vent.

In 'A' flight we had learnt to work together, to safeguard each other, and ultimately to rely each on the other; the governing spirit behind it all being a rigid self-discipline which emanated from Mick's own ardour. Such was the strength of the real fighting discipline in the Squadron that when Zulu Lloyd, Mick, Keen, Tudhope or I met over the lines, any one of us could unassumingly take the lead in an attack and the others would follow, only interested in the efficient waging of the war.

With us, seniority and prestige did not enter into the question as it would have done in the infantry or amongst non-fighting forces behind the lines.

In the air, the mutual respect of seasoned and enthusiastic fighters allowed them to rise to heights of self-discipline that could hardly have been conceived by any other unit of the fighting forces, a discipline so unorthodox that the senior pedants did their utmost to decry what they called 'Trenchard's undisciplined mob'.

An amusing side of this attitude was that very many of us had served two or three years surrounded by the strict discipline of infantry regiments. These pilots knew that the ordinary text-books were quite inadequate to meet even the first principles of air fighting, far less capable of inculcating the spirit the G.O.C. in France tried to foster.

Another aspect of the type of fighting that was carried on both in 1917 and 1918 was the terrifying casualty lists. In face of these it could be taken for granted that everyone who aspired to become a pilot, or observer, had at least a modicum of the spirit that could develop him into a fighter. The heavy death roll was debited to the lack of training, of flying ability, but on the other hand I noticed that the longer a pilot had spent in training at home before gaining some fighting experience, the more likely he was to be reported missing after a short period of actual fighting.

The real omission in the training curriculum was on the subject of the psychology and tactics of fighting much more than in the technicalities of flying or even formation flying.

It was a notorious fact that the majority of the really trained fliers, being filled with the aggressive spirit, thought that aerial fighting was merely a matter of shooting and stunting. What they failed to realise, and no one could blame them, was that it takes several weeks, if not months, of 'flirting' with death, to key the senses up to the alertness that formed a bulwark round experienced fighting pilots.

When a pilot did ultimately reach this stage it was merely a matter of a few months before the nervous strain began to affect his constitution. If he were kept at it too long, fearing the weakening of his own spirit, he was frequently tempted to carry out foolhardy enterprises by way of proving to himself that the 'spirit' was still there. In such a nervous condition many really courageous pilots met their deaths, the esprit survived, but the senses had been blunted, and — we were hard up for seasoned fighters.

With the ordinary pilot this defect was usually remedied by a change of two or three months. Mick had shown several signs of 'cracking-up' in November and December 1917, but on his return to France in April 1918 his nerves had so far recovered that he brought down over forty German machines in a space of two and a half months.

This remarkable success acted as a still greater inspiration to those he had instructed and to whom he had imparted some of his 'fire' and patriotism. The governing feature of his training, however, had been the 'nursing' of the promising material on which he had had to work. So great was Mannock's genius and influence that between the two flights he commanded in 40 and 74 Squadrons, over eighty conquests were obtained with the loss of only two pilots, Kennedy in '40' and Dolan in '74'. His two most outstanding pupils were J. Ira Jones of '74' (popularly known as 'Taffy') who won the D.S.O., M.C., D.F.C. and M.M., and G. E. H. McElroy (McIrish) who before his death was awarded the M.C. (two bars) and D.F.C. (one bar). Both were spirited, aggressive fighters, and as had been the case with McElroy on the occasion of his first victory the trouble was not to encourage them but to restrain and protect them until experience had allowed them to show their superiority over the more expert of the enemy fighters. Those who came most under Mick's influence are the first to pay tribute and to acknowledge their indebtedness to him for his example, his tuition and his care.

In our first weeks of fighting both of us had undergone a gruelling which very quickly persuaded us that aggressiveness must be accompanied by a constant and alert watchfulness. Mick made sure that his pupils were given the chance to develop the latter. His attitude towards us was that of brotherly affection, tempered by a true conception of war economics.

One incident, typical of the attitude Mick adopted to young and promising pilots, took place just before he went on leave in December 1917. It was the practice to send us off in pairs, and on this occasion Mick and Wolff had to go together. After their leave warrants arrived, Mick saw that Wolff had to go up on patrol and, because of the very popular superstition that it was almost suicidal to go over the lines with a leave ticket in one's pocket, Mick made up his mind that he would act as 'fairy godmother' to 'C' flight. Throughout the four beats of the patrol, Mick's S.E.5 was to be seen behind the flight and almost two thousand feet above Wolff, the surest way of safeguarding the 'warrant holder'.

It was consideration like this that earned Mannock the affection and loyalty of all those with whom he came in close contact. The intensity of his humanity and sympathy roused reciprocal feelings in others and, when in '40', even to the Germans as individuals he showed an extreme consideration and admiration as strong in the one direction as was his hatred for the organisation for which they were fighting in the other.

During the war I failed to understand the German mentality. They were undoubtedly brave individually, their organisation was almost perfect, yet collectively they lacked the spirit that could so easily have maintained the aerial supremacy won for them by the Fokker monoplane in 1915. Their much-admired 'system' was deficient in one essential feature; their pilots, both officers and N.C.O.s, were tied too strictly by discipline of the wrong sort. The German higher command failed to appreciate what our headquarters in France had very quickly realised, that the greatest weapon a fighter pilot possessed was his spirit. The enemy's systematised training and fighting failed to gain for him what our greater freedom did for us.

Even in 1918, when the results of the intensive German manufacture of machines and training of pilots were brought to fruition, and patrols of from fifteen to fifty enemy machines were to be encountered, our pilots continued to fly many miles over hostile country, perpetrating considerable damage on enemy communications and supports. Had the German pilots been allowed greater freedom of action they might have put a stop to this and have saved their ground forces a great deal of demoralisation and destruction. With our more elastic method, backed up by pilots who had been trained to think and act on their own responsibility, the British easily proved themselves the victors in the air.

*

Since then it has been my fortune to have as friends several of the pilots against whom 'A' flight frequently fought. They themselves do not lack the spirit, it was their system that denied it to them, the cruel, inhuman, machine that took everything from a fighter including his individuality. We called it Hunnishness.

Now, however, the German Air Force is being reconstructed on entirely different lines. Their principal bulwarks in the future will be tradition and spirit. They have changed their 'system', the new patriotic German movement has seen to that. Richthofen Squadrons have been formed; promising fighters have been carefully selected and placed under the tuition of the men who did the fighting in Richthofen's famous circus and similar Jagdstaffeln. These experienced pilots being now liberated from the cast-iron rigidity of Prussianist discipline are trying to build squadrons in the method which Mannock and Caldwell did in No. 74 Squadron.

*

Meanwhile, having been attacked by every nonentity who can wield a pen, by those whose horizon is bounded by 'Military Law' and 'Infantry Training', our R.A.F. shows signs of succumbing to the demoralising and uninspired system pursued by the Germans during the war. According to such writers everything British was wrong; our Generals were inefficient, our organisation was inadequate. Recriminations in the worst possible taste have been made in newspapers, magazines and books, resulting in the development of an *inferiority complex*, which in turn has caused our authorities to copy the methods of other nations, particularly the German. Our ex-enemies, to return the compliment, are doing their best to simulate the spirit demonstrated by us during the war.

One of the most pronounced features of this *inferiority complex* on our part has been the amazing amount of publicity that has been given to the German ace Richthofen and the almost entire absence of any real interest in our own fighters. The average Britisher has been persuaded that the only Air Force of any account was the *German*, and that it was exceedingly reckless (if courageous) of our pilots to venture near the lines.

This demoralising and subversive propaganda that has been carried on by all types of writers, both serious and sensational, has been allowed to germinate only because of the unassuming nature of the pilots who knew how false were the assumptions on which the writers based their stories.

In his inspiring biography of Mannock, *King of Air Fighters*, the author, Squadron Leader Jones, D.S.O., M.C., D.F.C., M.M., who, in my opinion, is our leading ace, has given an accurate account of Mannock's life and of the real position in France. The book refutes these false beliefs concerning air fighters and, in giving graphic descriptions of the fighting in 74 Squadron, deals with the modesty, conscientious workmanship, and idealistic patriotism of Major Edward Mannock, V.C., D.S.O. (two bars), M.C. (one bar), the lovable, sympathetic, energetic Captain of 'A' flight. From a very humble origin Mick rose to heights of patriotism in individual effort, in organisation and in leadership, that were unequalled by any of the fighters on either side of the lines.

*

Printed in Great Britain
by Amazon

84802331R00116